# MY TIME WITH META GIVEN
## Biography

### Herstory
Author, Journalist, Editor, Home Economist, Photographer, Consultant, Syndicated Columnist, Teacher, Scientist

## DANETTE BISHOP MONDOU

Copyright © 2018 Danette Bishop Mondou

All rights reserved.

Please note that all content within this book is the exclusive rights of Danette Bishop Mondou. No part here within shall be used without explicit permission by the author. If you have questions or queries, please inquire through the author page. Thank you for your interest and patience.

**Danette Bishop Mondou/Publisher**
**South Windsor, Connecticut**

Publisher's Note: This is a work of non-fiction.

ISBN-10: 7325876-1-2
ISBN-13: 978-1-7325876-1-8

Dedication to my family through all the generations!

*"For of all sad words of tongue or pen,
The saddest are these:
'It might have been!'"*

— John Greenleaf Whittier

# Contents

Introduction .................................................................................................. v
    The Journey ............................................................................................. v
Chapter One ................................................................................................. 1
    The Early Years ........................................................................................ 1
Chapter Two ................................................................................................. 9
    The Family ............................................................................................... 9
Chapter Three ............................................................................................ 23
    One Hundred and Thirty Years in the Making ................................... 23
Chapter Four .............................................................................................. 40
    Dynamic Duo ......................................................................................... 40
    Carrie and Meta from bio articles ........................................................ 40
Chapter Five ............................................................................................... 67
    The Cookbook ....................................................................................... 67
Chapter Six ............................................................................................... 106
    **From the Encyclopedia** ................................................................... 106
Chapter Seven .......................................................................................... 141
    Meta Given and the Women of Her Time ........................................ 141
Chapter Eight ........................................................................................... 162
    Meta's Life and Times ......................................................................... 162
Chapter Nine ............................................................................................ 170
    What about women, where did Meta fit in? ..................................... 170
Chapter Ten .............................................................................................. 186
    Meta Given's Dominance with Women, 1925-1949 ......................... 186
Chapter Eleven ......................................................................................... 212
    The Art of Cooking and Better Meals .............................................. 212
Chapter Twelve ........................................................................................ 224
    Careers .................................................................................................. 224
Timeline ................................................................................................... 263
Given Family Tree from 1693 – 1981 ..................................................... 267
Bibliography ............................................................................................. 268
Index ......................................................................................................... 275

# Introduction

## The Journey

THIS journey began a long time ago. It started with the purchase of the *Meta Given's Modern Encyclopedia of Cooking* by my mother and her sister in 1953. Then came all the meals, the family gatherings, and dishes.

Years go by with little or no notice of whom was guiding the nutrition in our families. Mother's research into "how bread was made" (while my sister learned to walk) or the purchase of vegetables were all taken for granted. We overlooked who was giving the invaluable information to our caregivers until now.

Then I started noticing my mother always calling her cookbook "Meta Given." My mother and her sister were referencing a very large green book. From this wonderful book came the creamed eggs on toast in the dark when the lights went out. There was the hot cocoa on a cold winter's day with warm butter toast cut in three or four strips for easy dunking.

Potato salads were a main staple mostly from spring to fall of every year. They graced the table with beans and warm rolls. There were discussions about whether to put or not put the onions in the salad. If Dad was around, no onions, if not, then let the onions be. However, if my aunt was making the salad there was no discussion, in went the onions and my father would eat as if it was the best salad ever.

Then around 2010 I watched a movie called *Julie & Julia*. This movie was the seed that eventually propelled this book. I started a cooking blog, but I was unsuccessful in keeping it up daily. I have a job that needs at least fifty hours a week of my time. I managed to write a few stories about our experiences with the food from the Meta Given cookbook.

By this time, I was going to do a bio piece of Meta Given. When I discussed the prospect with my mother, she thought you could not publish such a piece without permission. So, I did nothing for about one year. Then I met my cousin Katherine's son Joseph, the writer. I read pieces of one of his books. And I said, by Jove if he can write, so can I.

I had wanted to write a book but could never really settle on a subject. Then Meta Given guided me through her life for the next five years. I would research, write, do more research, and write some more. Until finally, I had her life's story in the form of a book.

The hard part came along. The rewriting, the editing, and what to include and what not to include. It has been quite the journey. But Meta Given and Danette Mondou have been having the time of their lives rehashing the life and times of Meta.

She has had her secrets that she has given up through one webpage after another. Most of the information came in drips and drabs. But when I discovered newspapers.com, well then, the information flowed like the Missouri River on a rainy day in spring.

Meta had a very rich and rewarding life. With a twenty-two-year teaching career, a twenty-four-year career as a home economist with over sixteen years as a consultant with her own business, and another thirty years as an author of cookbooks.

We came together through my mother, and eventually the Internet would bring alive this wonderful woman whose life was almost completely obliterated from the face of the earth if it had not been for her books. The Internet provided wonderful information through multiple websites like newspapers.com, Google, Fulton Post Cards and so many others. I would have been lost without the Internet for this daunting project.

I have been able to find references to her full career from as early as 10 years of age when she started concocting her own recipes until her books went out of print at age eighty-four. Lest we forget this wonderful woman's life and times, she single-handedly fed a nation.

Meta guided my research for the past five years. She watched over my shoulder as I started my journey. She championed me on and goaded me when I was stuck. For instance, I knew that her name was Meta H. Given. But it would be several months before I obtained knowledge of her middle name. I only found that out through her transcript at the University of Chicago.

Little tidbits of information like this eluded me sometimes for months. Then all of a sudden there it would be, on a page for me to see. The elation of learning about each and every piece of her life has been so very exciting and rewarding. There are still little pieces that I do not know. Many things I am sure I will never know. But I feel satisfied with what I have learned. I have put her career timeline together from the beginning to the end (see Timeline).

Meta never forgot many lesson that she imparted to us such as the reason for 50 pages in the *Modern Encyclopedia of Cooking* on how to make basic white bread. My mother lovingly taught the neighbor girl how to make bread using those thorough instructions.

Meta touched all our lives in ways we can only imagine. I have read story after story of how she has touched so many lives with her recipes, her instructions, her ability to share her home and leftover food with people who were down and out on their luck.

I understand why Jane Nickerson wished to do the interview. Jane came into her career at the tail end of Meta Given's career. Meta may have been one of her heroes. Jane was the Food Editor for the *New York Times*.

I like Jane Nickerson wished to pay homage to one of her fellow food editors. Why not? After all there were are women food editors left.

This is the story of a woman, a simple and humble woman who is wrapped in a 100-year history. It is not about someone who fell in and out of love unless you mention food. It is about someone who had lived a determined life. An important purpose of life. That life was worth living, reliving and certainly retelling.

This may not be your typical biography. However, I have called this labor of love *My Time with Meta Given* because it encompasses more than just Meta Given's life. I have tried to put down everything that I discovered about Meta, the different times that she lived through and other women who I discovered along the way.

I know that biographies are supposed to follow some rules, however, I believe that they also should be surrounded by the world and history of their lives. Biographies have always been one of my favorite reads. Two books that influenced my choices are *Tuesday's with Morrie* and *Julie & Julie*.

I also could not help throwing in stories I thought of while I was writing this book. I know this is not my story, but Meta has been with me for over 60 years and this was our time. I spent the best part of five years writing, research and rewriting this book. I couldn't help but jump in once in a while.

# Chapter One

## The Early Years

*Dedicated to my Great Grandmother Florence*

META Given moved through ninety-three years of life. She was born in 1888. But I have a feeling that the life she lived, at least from about 1888 to 1900, was further back in time. She says she grew up in a three-room homesteader's cabin.

In 1888, as with many times in life, there are those who live hard lives and those who have an easier time. Meta Given's family falls on the side of having a tough time as opposed to the easy life.

She remembered the hearth that the family sat around and the crackle of the fire. Toasting marshmallows by the fire, not really — but making dinner and warming by the fire on a cold winter's night. Making dinner consisted of roasting a bird from a string all day. She talked about the lives of her grandmothers' personal experience.

This is how she learned about cooking, which came down through the generations. From word of mouth and from hand to hand, at the elbow of the previous generation like her mother learned. Were there hardships and sorrows?

Yes! When you live in a log cabin with only the hearth to warm you, you spend every spare moment chopping wood for the long cold winters. Every meal needs to be caught, picked, or chopped by hand.

There are no shortcuts. There are no prepared meals at the grocer. There are no frozen cutlets, or already canned fruits and vegetables. Each item is planted, harvested, and preserved by you and your family and hired hands if you can afford them.

Meta's ancestral family were slave owners; however, by 1886, when her parents married, slavery was abolished through a harsh and horrific civil war. It tore the nation apart. The war was family against family, neighbor against neighbor. There were no true winners for many years.

Meta's family did have farm hands to assist with the arduous work. That does not mean they sat on the front porch and observed. It only meant that they were able to lighten their load. Meta Given's family consisted of mother, father, and two daughters.

It was a time when all clothing was made by hand sewing, wool shearing, cotton gathering and spinning and then knitting or weaving. Many family members knew how to knit or weave. If you wanted dinner, the wife prepared dinner with the daughters' help, while the father picked up the knitting where Mother left off.

Sewing included warm rugs on the bare floor with straw as a cushion. Curtains made of newspaper were upgraded from store-bought cloth (Post-Dispatch, 1941).

Education is very precious and a way to a brighter future. Meta's family believed in education; therefore, both of the Given girls got an education, which included normal schools with teaching certificates. These certificates allowed them to make a living while they attended high school as early as fourteen years of age.

If you injured yourself, most of those injuries were treated by Dr. Mom. Something as minor as a little cut of the finger could be near fatal. Walking in the fields. Sharpening axes. Maintaining wagons. Caring for horses. Milking cows. All dangerous work. One false move, one careless motion could end your life or cause permanent injures.

Not much is known about Meta's daily life, but how difficult Meta's life may have been. Most of what I am relaying comes from her own writings and biography pieces in newspapers or in her cookbooks.

For Meta, everything sounds rosy and great. She talks about how much easier things are for some people today (for her, 1925-1950), but she seldom goes into much detail. However, we know from other people's accounts of the Midwest about taming the land, disagreements with the Native Americans, and more or less life in general was hard and arduous work. And there was seldom time for doing nothing.

If you went to school, there were chores before and after. Animals were fed, milked, and groomed. Gardens were tended, meals prepared, and you could never let an idle moment go by where you weren't chopping wood. We take this life we live today for granted. Turn on a light. Set that heat to whatever temperature you want and what's for dinner? "Reservations!"

Need a new one of that? "Alexa, put it on my order." There were no restaurants close by. No local grocer to peruse for prepared foods. You want cereal, granola, cookies, cakes and pies? You better be prepared to make them.

There were days of harvesting, which were then followed with preserving the food – cold storage, jams and jellies and the like. And if you wanted meat, then you better know how to kill, dress, bleed and cut it, and then preserve it if possible.

Most nights you go to bed so exhausted you are sure you won't be able to wake up the next day. If you did, you were unable to move. Milking started at 4:00 a.m., before breakfast and during all of this, you better be chopping the wood.

There was laundry on Monday, every Monday. That meant carrying the water, heating the water, then soaking your clothes overnight.

Saturday night was bath night. Again, with the carrying of water, bringing in the tub. Once you got cleaned, you got out quickly, as rooms were colder. Houses were drafty. Yes, it was difficult, but Meta was a hard worker who came from hearty stock.

Then the cleanup, and possibly a social gathering at the local community center that doubled as the schoolhouse, town meeting place and the evening dance spot on Saturday. You may have been privileged to have a separate building as a church or the same community building.

Women often did the bulk of the water-carrying work. They walked hundreds of miles in a year in pursuit of water. Many people were not lucky enough to have a pump in their home from the well. If you had a well, you would go and fetch the water and carry it back to the house.

So, if you want to know why bath night was once a week, it was due to having to carry the water, not to mention all the other chores during the week. You all shared the same bath.

In the movies, you see how romantic it is to have a bath drawn for you. Be assured, there was a lot of work involved, with the bulk being performed by the women.

Meta would learn to multitask, as all women do. She cooked dinner for herself and her farm hands and her dad one day when her mother scooted over to help a sick neighbor. This was not a problem for Meta, who was nine years old.

Dinner consisted of a freshly killed and plucked turkey, thick and tart wild gooseberry sauce made for filling a sweet yellow cake recipe she got from the *Journal of Agriculture* cookbook. Throughout these endeavors, she most likely had to carry all the water needed for the day, keep the stove stoked and set the table.

It is believed that it took about four hours a day, every day to manage the stove. We are not sure if Meta had a stove this early on. Most homesteader log cabins would have had a hearth instead of a stove.

Meta repeated many times that she was concocting her own recipes by the age of ten. She claims there was very little variety in their diets.

Therefore, Meta felt the need to concoct her own recipes to give the same-old, same-old some pizazz.

In 1941 on January 2, a beautiful bio piece ran in the *St. Louis Post-Dispatch* out of St. Louis, Missouri. This article is not credited to anyone specific; however, the person who wrote the article was able to give us a snapshot of Meta Given, her life and her times.

Meta was raised on a small farm in a log cabin that had lime chinking for the cracks. They didn't have a lot, but her mother provided a handmade woven rag rug that was used in the winter months to warm the floor with a wagon load of wheat straw that Meta claims made for great somersaults.

Sounds like her parents were free thinkers who enjoyed their children by letting them play in the house during the cold winter months. Her mother also provided scalloped window shades made from newspaper until they could afford store-bought cloth for curtains.

Meta told about her hobbies. In 1941 she hadn't much time for hobbies by then. But her favorites were horseback riding and rowing. Accomplishments as a college girl included rowing one of those activities outside of book studies.

Meta Given started working on her career as early as ten years old, according to this and many other articles and introductions to her cookbooks. She would hone her craft of the experimental kitchen while teaching at schools such as Brookfield and Flat River.

While at Brookfield, she perfected a home economics course that did not go unnoticed by the superintendent of schools. When the superintendent left Brookfield to go to Flatbed, he tapped her to run the newly formed home economics program. This program was created through her innovation.

There she was the Head of the Home Economics Department where she fine-tuned her classes in a special hall that was built at Flatbed.

In 1914, she went to the University of Chicago which included classes at the Universities of Missouri and Wisconsin rounding out her education in home economics. Her humble and difficult beginnings drove her as she worked her way through college while simultaneously teaching and developing one of the best home economic departments at Flatbed.

As I read the article, I marvel at the amount of work she was able to accomplish. She simultaneously worked as a chemistry teacher, a laboratory chemistry assistant to a professor and was a student at Warrensburg Normal School #2, which would later become one of the state teachers' colleges.

I wonder if Meta felt like going to school, teaching and being a laboratory assistant was easier than the work she had to accomplish on the farm? I know that there is a big leap from doing farm work to doing school work, especially college.

Not everyone can make that leap, however, both Meta and her sister Carrie were able to be successful in their school work. They both became teachers as well as furthered their careers, one as a home economist and the other as a High School Principal (uncommon in 1926, with men occupying the majority of the principal jobs). In 2017 things have changed a little, while 76 percent of teachers are women, you still only have 52 percent women as principals.

Meta and her sister were two very strong women who went after what they wanted. Neither of them seemed to shy away from challenging work, whether that work was on the farm, in a classroom or as professionals. The leaps they made in their lives are to be applauded and honored by history.

# Chapter Two

## The Family

*Dedicated to Leola Gerow Bishop – love of family and cooking!*

META Given came from an extensive line of Irish descent. Her great-grandfather nine generations back was Scottish.

Her great-grandfather was named Henry Given and her great-grandmother was Charity Boggs Given. They lived in Virginia until 1858, when three generations of the Scotch-Irish family packed their belongings, loaded wagons, acquired what money they could gather and headed for Missouri.

Or maybe they left by stagecoach, as was advertised in the Richmond Dispatch on a regular basis informing the potential traveler how fast travel was by coach. These advertisements tried to entice them with all the wonderful stops along the way (Virginia Springs, 1856).

In addition, there were trains which left the Richmond area to all points. All and any modes of transportation could be used to take them to their future destination. Which mode or modes of transportation the Given families chose is left up to our imaginations.

There's no one left to tell their story of how or exactly why Meta Given's ancestors left the Virginia area, but it seems like there was an exodus of (West) Virginians, as was reported in the October first edition of the 1856 Richmond paper about "West Virginians (West Virginians, 1856)."

There was a plea as to why there may have been a mass exodus of people from Virginia. The only destination area they mentioned in the 1856 article of the *Richmond Dispatch* was New York. However, there must have been people leaving for Missouri as well, for this is the place where the Given's family landed.

*The Richmond Dispatch* also reported on the crops in Missouri, as well as other parts of the country. Wheat, hemp and apples were all crops of the day from Missouri. Family conversations must have consisted of how they could make a fine living in the Ozarks of Missouri.

Between their farming knowledge and other endeavors in Virginia, this knowledge equated well in Missouri. So, they packed their belongings, loaded up their wagons and headed to Missouri for land that was available through land grants.

In 1856 and even in 1858 there was no West Virginia. Therefore, there may be some confusion when looking at her family census data. Some references say their family was from Virginia, and others say they were from West Virginia. The state did not separate into two states until the civil war around 1863. This separation occurred over slavery and other volatile subjects of the day.

It is the best reason the Given family packed up three generations (a clan) and moved to Missouri. Missouri was a newly formed slave state, causing a stir and creating the Missouri Compromise around 1820. You may have heard of the Mason-Dixon line.

Well, the Missouri Compromise created its own line called the "Missouri Line."

Both lines defined the North as non-slave states and the South as slave-states. However, if you observe the location of Missouri, it is smack dab in the middle of the line that separates the north from the south. Hence the need for the Missouri Compromise and the line from Missouri all the way to the West Coast. This was rescinded in 1857 by the Kansas-Nebraska Act, which opened further territories for slavery.

The Given family were slave owners at least as far back as when William Given was alive in the 1780s. According to William's will, he had slaves he bequeathed to his family at the time of his death in 1792.

The Irish trace their heritage through Northern-Ireland in the Given family, specifically the Antrim County of Ireland. England encouraged Scottish Lowland Presbyterians to migrate to the Ulster area of Ireland to strengthen its control of England and increase the Presbyterian population of Ulster.

There were many groups of Irish who came to the colonies from as early as 1720 through the 1800s. Meta Given's family was not specifically associated with any of these groups, as they arrived in 1738 after the 1720 William Penn group and before the 1763-1775 migration, where 55,000 Scotch-Irish from Ulster arrived along with some 40,000 Scots.

They migrated to Virginia, distancing themselves from many other groups. They were probably part of the Scotch-Irish Planters, as they strongly believed in slavery and its ability to build the colonies while creating wealth for the King of England.

The Scotch-Irish turned their lives toward the West which included Tennessee, Kentucky and finally the Ozarks of Missouri and Arkansas.

Missouri found itself continually switching sides throughout the years before and through the Civil War. (thelibrary.org site) they "held Missouri for the old flag." "Old flag" references the Northern non-slave beliefs.

Also, there was some references to how they wore the hearts on their sleeve. As there was very little hugging and such where even if they had not seen each other in years, a shake of the hand and a howdy was enough even between mother and child. More than that might be an embarrassment for both parties.

"There is a myriad of possible reasons for the immigration of so many of the Scots-Irish to America in the 1700s. High rents and religious persecution have often been blamed. Most of the Scots-Irish came freely to the American colonies, although there were also some who were deported as prisoners or came as indentured servants. Others came with British Army regiments and remained in the American colonies."

Within the research of the Irish or Scots-Irish there is much speculation, but I feel none of this pertained to Meta Given's ancestors. Samuel Given came at the request of King George II, therefore, there was no high rent or religious persecution.

"The Scots-Irish largely came to colonial America in family groups. They came as members of an extended family settled near one another in America, whether they immigrated together or separately."

You can see this is true with Meta Given's family. Not only did they come with their full family, if you look at the people Samuel Given's children married, many of the second generation's spouses were from Ulster County, Ireland.

*Meta Given's Family 7 Generations (Family Tree)*

Taking a closer look at the long and wonderful family lineage of Meta, James, Henry, and all the way back before Samuel, even to the time of Hugh Given:

The first generation in the American Colonies, Samuel Given (Meta's fifth-great-grandfather) was born in 1693 in Antrim Ulster County, Ireland. He was the generation which marked the beginning of Meta's American heritage.

The first to come to this country from Ireland, Samuel brought his nine children and wife Sarah with him. He was commissioned by the King of England George II to be one of three magistrates of the largest county in the Colony of Virginia.

While this family I tell about is not my family, they are Meta Given's family. I am sure she missed her grandmother and many others when they passed away. Meta was only four years old when her paternal grandmother left her and her family on January 11, 1892 at the age of eighty.

Then Meta lost her beloved father James Henry Given on March 29, 1920. He passed away soon after the 1920 census, right after his sixty-second birthday. All the rest of her days she mourned his death, but she honored him as she told us stories about his appreciation of food she learned so well at her joyous family's table.

Losing her mother came quite a long time after her father's death, as her mother lived to be about eighty-three years old. She is buried next to her beloved husband, with a date of death marker of April 11, 1949. Meta enjoyed the company of her mother for sixty-one years of Meta's life. Ann Given, Meta's mother, passed away while they were vacationing in Florida.

Meta's mother was there to support her throughout Meta's long and illustrious career. As Meta's career began to wind down, she loses her mother but, in her passing, there was the sorrow and the laughter. We miss those who go before us, we feel their presence once they are gone in a way we did not feel it while they were living, giving us the belief, they are with us every day, everywhere.

Sometimes we feel the presence of those who have gone before us even when we did not know them directly. It may be a grandmother or a grandfather who could be from several generations before. I wonder how much Meta Given knew about her greats, the many generations before.

Most family histories are passed along from one generation to another. However, the most one might know is from stories told through the generations by word of mouth.

Some of these stories can be invoked by an item in the household, a piece of farm equipment, even a dress or a measuring cup. Look around your house and you will find an item belonging to someone who came before.

It could be a gift given at a holiday or on your birthday. These items hold special memories. When you touch them, they bring alive the person they belonged to in the past or the person who gave them to you.

I have unearthed such information about Meta Given's family going back some eight generations and beyond, possibly. Through research, I have been able to discover one Samuel Given, who at the age of forty-five, with his nine children and wife Sarah Cathey of Antrim County, Ulster, Ireland immigrated to the largest county in the Americas, called Orange County, which was in Virginia.

What a brave thing to do, this crossing of the Atlantic Ocean with your family for a land still growing. Going into the unknown, or at least only known through stories and newspaper articles of the romance of the Americas.

Samuel Given, the future magistrate of the largest county in the American colonies, was born in 1693 to one Samuel Given of Scotland in the Ulster area of Northern Ireland. He was born during the land-grabbing days of the late 1600s.

The Given family moved at the request of King Henry VIII to Ulster, Ireland. The King hoped to even the odds, to persuade the Catholic Irish to be more loyal by placing Presbyterian believers in their realm. As we all know, King Henry VIII threw out the Catholic religion to divorce Queen Catherine of Aragon, who had not produced an heir.

King Henry VIII needed a son and heir, and he moved heaven and earth to make this happen. This move aligned Samuel Given's family with the Kings of England.

Samuel Given becomes one of three magistrates in Orange County, Virginia, commissioned by the King of England, George II. He moved his family under his own expense, first going to Pennsylvania then traveling to Virginia.

Samuel and Sarah had nine children from the ages of 19 to three when they moved to the American Colonies.

Samuel signed importation papers dated August 23, 1739. This affidavit was necessary for him to hold property. He purchased 311 acres of land known as Beverly Manor for seven pounds, ten shillings and sixpence from William Beverly in 1738. This became the home of Samuel Given and his family, where he lived and died. Samuel is buried in the cemetery at Old Stone church in Fort Defiance, Virginia.

All of Samuel Given's children were born in Antrim Co. Ulster, Ireland, except for the youngest, George Given, born in 1740 in Virginia in Augusta County after the death of his father, Samuel.

Meta Given's family line goes from Samuel who came here from Ireland to his first-born son, who became Captain John Given. John Given was a captain in the Muster of Augusta Co., Virginia in 1742. John (Meta's fourth great-grandfather) was born in Ireland and came to the colonies with his father, mother and siblings in 1738.

Captain John was a soldier and fought in the American Revolution. John was a landowner, merchant, tanner, constable, road overseer, and a captain in the Revolutionary War. He was captain of a militia under his uncle, General Andrew Lewis, in the battle of Point Pleasant.

He also served with Colonel John Boyer's Regiment, and in Campbell's Brigade under Lafayette, and was with Col. Robertson when Tarleton plundered Charlottesville. During his career, he was promoted to major. But he was always referred to as Captain John.

William Given (Meta's third great-grandfather) was born to Captain John and wife Mary in Augusta County, Virginia on March 21, 1746.

William's will of 1792 read "...to wife Nancy, her bed and furniture and all bed clothes, the best horse or mare that I have that she will choose."

William Given II (Meta's second great-grandfather) born June 18, 1773 in Bath County, he is the next in line in the Meta Given family. He married Virginia Jane Frame, who was born on a fall day, October 3, 1774, in Bath County, Virginia.

They started their lives together on December 16, 1792 in Braxton County, Virginia. William and

Virginia had nine children. William and Nancy were the parents of Henry Given.

Henry Given (Meta's great-grandfather) was born in 1808 in Braxton County. He is the next generation in the family of Meta Given. Henry married his beloved Charity L. Boggs, who was born in 1811 in Braxton County, Virginia.

Henry and Charity had six children the first was John C. Given, born 1829. Henry Given died many years later on March 17, 1887, long after they moved from Virginia to Missouri. Henry Given passed away in Paydown, Maries County, Missouri, and his final resting place is at Johnson cemetery in Maries County.

John C. Given (Meta's grandfather) the firstborn of Henry and Charity, is the next in the extensive line of the Given family. He was born 1829 in Braxton County, Virginia, and married Elizabeth Baker, who was born in 1835. John and Elizabeth are the grandparents of Meta Given.

They married in 1850 in Wirt County Virginia, district 70. John and Elizabeth had two children, Louisa J. Given born 1851, and Lenora A. Given born in 1855 before they moved to Missouri. James Henry Given was born 1858 in Missouri soon after they arrived from Virginia. Henry, Charity and their children and their children's children all move to Missouri. Three generations in all.

James Henry Given, born on November 9, 1858 in Missouri, was the son of John C. and Elizabeth. James married Eliza Ann Lacy, who was born April 1, 1866. James and Eliza Lacy, who is also known as

Ann, married in 1887 in Missouri. Ann was twenty-one years of age. They lived in Bourbois Township, Gasconade County, Missouri, and had two children, Meta Hortense Given, born January 25, 1888, and Carrie Given, born March 1, 1890.

Ann's father was Levi Lacy, who was born on June 3, 1866 in Grainger, Tennessee. Levi married Eliza Ann Miller in 1829. They had nine children in thirty years. Levi died on January 23, 1866, in Gasconade, Missouri at the age of 59. This was Meta Given's maternal grandfather and grandmother.

James and Ann have two children, Meta and Carrie. Meta Given never married or had children, so the line of the Given family we followed first crossed the English Channel to Ireland from Scotland, then crossed the Atlantic Ocean from Ireland for the American colonies comes to the end of the line. Finally, they crossed hundreds of miles of various terrain from the state of Virginia to the state of Missouri, where the lineage died out with Meta.

Meta's younger sister Carrie married William Aufder Heide. They have no children together so the Given family line through this family lineage dies out. Carrie's husband had two sons from a previous marriage.

I have tracked the Given family from 1570 until the present day. Meta Given did her family proud by taking something everyone needs to sustain life and turning it into her life's work. Each generation worked hard to help the next generation along. The wills of Samuel and William show they believed in building enough wealth to pass it along to the next generation.

Both wills ensure provisions for the next generation and for the widows, so they could live in their homes "unmolested." This was not always the case in the 1700 and 1800s. While women found themselves at the mercy of the eldest male of the family for their future care and well-being, this was not the case for the Given women.

There was a lot of respect and consideration given to the women of the family. You could tell this by what the men provided after they were gone, through their wills. The Given family respect for women continued to Meta and Carrie. Meta Given goes to school from grammar to college graduate work. While she worked, all that time she was getting her education, so there must have been a lot of support during those years.

Meta Given was left land when her father passed away. There is mention in several articles in the Owensville newspaper about land transfers, land leasing and other articles regarding Meta Given's inheritance.

Henry and Charity, James Given's grandparents, moved to Missouri in 1858. There were many family meetings about moving out of Virginia for the sake and protection of the men, women, and children of the family. War is a very difficult business, and no good can come if there was a war. The Given family acclimated to Missouri very well, as they lived there for many generations.

Meta Given was not born when her grandfather died in 1885. However, she was alive while her grandmother Charity was still living, up to four years of Meta's life. Meta talked about her grandmother's influence on her when it came to the preparation of food as well as her mother's influence.

When mentioning food, Meta said she got her love of food from her father. It sounds like he enjoyed a delicious meal. Meta's mother Ann must have been a wonderful cook and teacher, as relayed to us through stories Meta Given tells about in her columns, books and articles written about Meta to promote her work. Meta's mother knew how to cook wonderful meals and present the food to the table in a pleasing, eye-catching way. These meals filled up all the senses.

Since Meta Given's great-grandparents Henry and Charity moved to Missouri with all the family, they probably had large family gatherings during the year. There were holidays, birthdays, weddings, deaths, barn raisings and many other occasions to have family gatherings. There is a mention of Meta and Carrie attending a family reunion gathering, which must have been one of many.

Meta Given mentioned they did not have a lot of money. However, I believe they were above average in their family holdings. Everyone owned their own homes and farms, and they did not have a mortgage. Each one of them appeared to have a little bit of money, about half of the price of their homes. These were nice little tidbits found in the U.S. Census in the mid-1800s.

While they may not have had extra money for luxury items, they had enough to purchase homes and put a little aside for a rainy day. They also had plenty when it came to the harvest of crops. They had apples, which Meta talked about in her articles. The state of Missouri and the Gasconade area were one of the largest growers of apples in the country, around the end of the nineteenth century.

Meta Given talked about not having a lot of variety with a bountiful harvest. It was up to her mother and eventually herself to prepare the family meals. Meta liked variety hence the need for many recipes for the same foods. Meta Given's education came from a variety of sources, such as her mother, father, grandparents, and school.

Meta Given's family was important to Meta's upbringing. They were there to help her form into the person she became, taking immense pride in her every accomplishment. Later in Meta's life, Meta, Carrie and their mother enjoyed many visits and even going on vacation to various locations, with Florida being one of their favorites.

Meta also honored her family with her stories and anecdotes in her articles and books. Everyone says each book we write will have a little bit of ourselves within the pages. Meta's autobiography is tucked safely within her books. The legacy of her and her family is just waiting to be read and discovered.

# Chapter Three

## One Hundred and Thirty Years in the Making

*Dedicate to all young-spirited girls!*

META'S life began over 130 years ago, when times were simpler. It was a time when our chores were performed more by hand and less by machine. Her life is worth remembering and cherishing for being a girl, a young woman, and a leader for all time. She was cherished by her parents, her audience and her students of life from 1888 until this very day. Please sit back and enjoy the journey as I have enjoyed it, discovering the fascinating and awesome life and times of none other than Meta Given.

A beautiful baby girl was born, Meta Hortense Given, on January 25, 1888 in the Ozarks of Missouri. She told of being born and growing up in a three-room cabin. This cabin was kept warm in the winter with a rug her mother made. Before the rug was placed upon the floor, a bed of straw was strewn about to increase the cushion and warmth. Meta said it was nice to step upon when first laid down and provided much fun until the straw cushion was matted down.

She was the first baby girl born to the excited and anxious parents of James and Ann Given on a small farm in rural Bourbois, Missouri. She was born during the coldest and snowiest of winters in recorded history. One of these storms in the winter of 1888 is the benchmark that all future storms have been compared to, up to this very day. As recent as 2015, there was a winter storm that would be noted as being right up there with the storm of 1888.

Right before and two months after Meta's birth, there were two horrific blizzards. The first on January 12, was called the School House Blizzard. It centered around the Great Plains of the United States, taking the lives of 235 people, many of them school-aged children as well as livestock, hurting the farmers deeply. This was not the worst of storms that year, just the most memorable in the minds of those who lost their dear ones.

The second storm is known as the "Great Blizzard of '88" on March 11-14 of 1888, which decimated the Eastern seaboard from Washington DC to Maine, taking more than 500 lives on land and sea. As you can see, it was a great time for the Given household, however, it was a scary time for much of the country.

Other storms were a-brewing in the United States. The suffrage movement may have stalled during the late 1800s, but it would pick up steam by the early 1900s. The suffrage movement was able to get the right to vote for women by 1920 with the help of people like Susan B. Anthony. Meta Given would not be one of our suffragettes, but she would benefit from the movement as this and many other changes move through her life.

Meta's parents James Henry and Elisa Ann (Lacy) Given would spend the next two years taking care of their baby girl until their second and last child arrived in 1890. They named her Carrie. The Givens' household was a prosperous home that spent their days teaching their children about farming, the care of crops and livestock and the multifaceted preparation of food.

In my mind's eye, I can see little Meta's beautiful red hair as it grows. It will grow into these long braids, at first being braided by her mother. Most likely, Meta would insist that she learn to do it herself. Eventually, the braids found their way into the crown on her head.

This crown was her signature hair style which served her well throughout her life. The crown became a necessity with all the cooking and farm work that needed to be done without the fuss of hair. Ultimately, it just became the way that Meta would wear her hair, so she could quickly get on with her day.

Meta was a tall woman for her time. The question arises: did she take after her mother or her father? I find that most people favor both. A little of the mother around the eyes and a little of the father around the forehead.

The funny thing is if you ask the mother, she will say she takes after the father. And if you ask the father he will say, she takes after her mother. We often don't see ourselves in our children. We see the beauty of the other parent in every little thing they accomplish. I like to believe she got the best of both.

This precocious girl, Meta Given, would learn quickly, and by the age of ten, she would be cooking and concocting her own recipes through the tutelage of her parents and grandparents. This knack and curiosity would shape the rest of her life and work.

Meta tells of a time when she was nine years old and had to cook a meal while her mother rushed off to assist a neighbor in need – possibly during the birth of a child. In her mother's absence, Meta had to cook a meal for her father and the farm hands. It turned out to be a turkey that had been killed by accident that morning by a wagon carrying wheat.

Their crops may have had a plentiful bounty, however, there was limitation in variety as Meta noted in her books and articles over the years. Little Meta Given's ever-expanding repertoire of recipes kept mealtime fun and interesting.

Meta must have been given a lot of latitude by her parents to allow her free rein with her concocted recipes at age ten. She may have kept a book of her recipes at the time, as it was the custom of many people to create and collect their own recipes in what was called a *receipt* book.

Yet another early accomplishment for this precocious girl is teaching grammar school at the age of 14. It seems that Meta Given was doing many things early. She tells of this on the jacket of her cookbooks and in an article written by Jane Nickerson, a Food Editor for the *Lakeland Ledger* and the *New York Times* many years later, in 1975.

Meta tells of moving from the three-room farmhouse to a town called Vienna, about twenty-five miles from where she grew up. She was thirteen years old. In this new town she was able to go to high school, pass an examination and teach school for the next five years.

Meta Given was born during the Second Industrial Revolution, specifically during the end of the Gilded Age (1878-1889). Meta lived during one of the biggest cooking revolutions, which included cookbooks and home economics.

One important part of the revolution had women requesting measuring utensils from the Blacksmith or the tin man to the mass production of standardized utensils from the factory. Much of this behavior can be observed at the Old Sturbridge Village in Massachusetts.

While Meta Given was learning farming and food preparation, Fannie Farmer (1857-1915) was publishing her first cookbook in 1896 called *The Boston Cooking-School Cook Book*. Fannie did not publish the first cookbook in America. That fame belongs to an orphan; Amelia Simmons, who wrote *American Cookery* published in 1798, around 100 years before Fannie's book of 1896. However, Fannie was the first to use standardized cooking utensils. She started this practice of uniform utensils starting in the mid-1800s.

There were many other revolutionizing inventions of the day, as Meta Given would lay witness to during her lifetime. These included the availability of the power of electricity or the telephone as it became obtainable, and the automobile as it developed from a novelty or luxury item to something the everyday person could afford and eventually not be able to live without.

These inventions led to so many other inventions that it might seem hard to keep up with all the technological advances at once (lights, fans, refrigerators, electrical plugs, toasters, coffee makers, washing machines, dishwashers, electric typewriters, etc.), far too many to list here. However, as with most inventions, they are slow to take hold and changes to society move at a such pace that the average person will take their sweet time to assimilate.

For instance, while millions of cars were rolling off the factory floor of the Ford Corporation, there were still many households that used the horse and wagon. While some towns and cities were getting electricity, there were others who still used their trusty oil lamps and handmade candles.

The same for the telephone installation: while it may become commonplace for larger cities or parts of the country, it would be years before another section would enjoy its conveniences. Often people found new technology intimidating, or they were suspicious of its impact on their lives.

Another invention that was making its mark in America as it swept the country in the 1800s was the "Normal School." This invention would affect the lives of women more than any other invention of the time. Education was power and a pathway to better-paying jobs. While they say women did not work outside of the home, many men did not either. There was a huge population of farmers with little or no formal education. Normal schools would change this for men and women alike.

Two important books have been written in the past couple of years to mark the importance of Normal schools. The first was written by Christine A. Ogren called *The American State Normal School, An Instrument of Great Good*. The other was called *The Bloomer*, which mentions women's roles in the sport of baseball and their participation in Normal schools.

Meta Given took advantage of an education at a local high school in the town of St. James. Meta enjoyed the benefits of going to school, when so many families opted not to have their daughters go at all and even some sons only finished grammar or middle school. Meta not only got a high school education but also was able to take advantage of the new Normal school education that swept the nation in the mid- to late-1800s.

Meta Given's education included three years of high school at St. James, which was about twenty miles from their home. She probably rented a room or stayed with relatives during the school year. She went to the high school from about 1905 through 1908, as listed on her transcript from the University of Chicago as a previous institution. Also, listed as a previous institution was the Warrensburg, (MO) State Normal School during 1912, which became the University of Central Missouri.

Normal schools were sweeping the United States from as early as 1823 when Samuel Read Hall founded the first in Concord, Vermont. Missouri would not start getting the Normal schools until the later part of the 1800s, with the Warrensburg School being founded in 1871 as the State Normal School District #2. This school being about 142 miles from her hometown, Meta would again find herself boarding in another town.

Meta Given was a member of this rich history of young women getting educated and working in the early part of the twentieth century. We find Meta Given started working before women got the right to vote in 1920, as the nineteenth Amendment (Amendment XIX) to the United States Constitution prohibits any United States citizen from being denied the right to vote on the basis of sex. This amendment did not get ratified until August 18, 1920.

With the nineteenth Amendment came other reforms of higher education, workplace professions and health care. The finances of Meta Given are not known before the vote of 1920. Some states allowed women to handle their own finances and some did not.

Meta Given helped pioneer a job for women as a school teacher. The country was very interested in providing a standardized "Normal" education to all children. In doing so, they were in desperate need for teachers. They wanted to standardize the education process, which they did with the Normal schools. Meta had obtained an education and was able to secure a teaching position initially as a grammar school teacher and eventually as a high school teacher and even working as a professor's assistant at Warrensburg.

Meta was a noted teacher of many subjects including science, math, agriculture, household arts, and physics. She also was the secretary representing Saint James for the South-Central Missouri School district out of Rolla, Missouri, documented in 1909 and 1910 through two different news articles, the latter in the *Springfield Republican newspaper* on November 23, 1910.

There were several resources documenting Meta Given's teaching career; one was the Patterson's American Education directory. This documentation shows the many teaching positions that Meta Given would hold over the years. Meta taught school from 1902 until 1922 at various schools. One of them was at Flat River teaching household arts in 1916. She would also teach at Brookfield High School in Brookfield, Missouri in the County of Linn in 1914. Another reference was in the Missouri State Teachers' Association Bulletin, volume 2-3.

It was during this time Meta Given felt that she needed extra education, so in 1914, when she was twenty-six years of age she matriculated at the University of Chicago.

During this time Henry Ford was perfecting his automobile, the Model T. Thomas Edison was getting his electricity installed in several cities across the nation, and the telephone was becoming so popular that in 1915 the first coast-to-coast long-distance call was made between Mr. Bell and Mr.

Watson. The Great War or World War I (WWI) was just getting started in Europe on July 28 of 1914.

Meta Given continued to teach and go to school while the rest of the world was inventing and reinventing the face of everyday life. She persevered and did not quit until she obtains her bachelor's degree in education in 1924. Meta did not go to school every semester as she was multitasking by teaching and learning simultaneously.

On July 26, 1920, the University of Missouri, also known as Warrensburg Normal, then the Central State Teacher's College, "holds a lawn banquet given by the Warrensburg Club on Dean Mumford's lawn, a hearty get-together. Miss Meta Given and Miss Etta McAlister were contestants to discover as many names of picnickers as possible within a few minutes allotted. Miss McAlister won through fleetness of foot rather than through actual count, over Miss Meta Given." This is one of many associations that Meta Given would belong to throughout her educational tenure.

Meta Given was the superhero that I thought she was. She spent her school semesters in the fall and in the spring teaching, then she would rush off to the summer semester starting in 1914 to study and take classes as a first-year student at the University of Chicago.

The education she acquired at Normal school gave her the ability to teach higher levels of education. Teaching was not enough for Meta. She needed more education to fill the gaps, especially regarding her scientific knowledge that she had gotten thus far.

She was willing to give up her summers from 1914-1922. Colleges allow you so much time to complete your degree. By 1922, Meta had been working on her bachelors for eight years. Quite possibly if she did not get her degree by 1924, she might have to take more courses or make some other change.

So, we find Meta going full-time by the autumn of 1923 with a completion in June of 1924. What a wonderful thing for Meta and her family as they witnessed Meta getting her Bachelor of Education degree from the University of Chicago at her graduation ceremony.

How exciting for her mother and her sister as they witnessed the moment when the Dean announces, "Meta Hortense Given," who walked on stage and got handed her diploma, with the moving of her tassel from one side of her graduation cap to the other as they do during the Pomp and Circumstance at graduations.

After the graduation, they would have enjoyed the taking of pictures, the congratulations and such. According to some research about the affection shown in Irish families, there may not have been hugs and kisses as they wore their hearts on their sleeves, but a handshake was enough of a public display with words of congratulations. They spoke louder with their eyes than any words or hugs could convey in their world.

What were the future plans from that moment for Meta, her sister and their mother? It was a turning point for Meta as well as the rest of the family during the years 1920–1926. Meta and Carrie's father passed away in 1920, bringing heartbreak as well as eventually turning them away from the family farm.

The girls both had jobs that took them away from the farm. Meta Given getting this degree would make her a home economist and open career possibilities that were an extension of her home economics teaching career of the past.

Where would the future lead for Meta? They may have discussed her furthering her career with graduate school and possibly getting a Ph.D. in home economics. They may have discussed Meta taking some time off. She had been working and going to school full-time since 1902 when she was fourteen, until now when she was thirty-six years old in 1924.

By 1925, Meta did start graduate school, and she got tapped for the first director's position at the Evaporated Milk Association in their home economics department, starting the first scientific kitchen. That would leave Carrie to make a dramatic move for herself. She had worked for several years as a principal in the local Owensville school system. They may have discussed how exciting it was for her to have such a great job.

Even as the principal, she still got to teach, and of course there were all the other activities: class plays to plan and coach. There was the senior banquet that the juniors put on for the seniors, and the work required to bring the students, staff and alumni together for a successful event.

Having a principal's job was a big deal, as those jobs generally went to men (In 1905, 95 percent of all high school principal jobs went to men). Carrie would hold that principal's position for four years. However, at the end of her third year she would make a dramatic move and marry. According to a little article in the Gasconade Republicanewspaper, Carrie married in secret, and her sister did not attend.

This choice would change her career life forever. She would lose her place as principal the next year, certainly having much to do with the fact that she was now married. The belief of the day was that married women did not need to work.

The principal's post did go to a man. However, she stepped in and helped when he left the principal job after one short year. She was much-loved in the town of Owensville, and at the school.

There may have been a discussion about what Mom should do for the future, possibly that Mom should live with Meta now that Dad had passed away. With how much work the farm required, maybe they could try to rent it out and make it easier on their mother and less worry for the girls.

As the summer turned into fall and fall into winter, Meta took the short walk into the registrar's office on a cold blustery day in January to sign up for graduate classes at the University of Chicago, not knowing that right around the corner was her first job opportunity to become the first director of the home economics department of a newly formed company called the Evaporated Milk Association.

Meta moved away from the education of children and young learners to the education of a nation. She spent five years educating a nation about the wonderful benefits of evaporated milk. Through her tireless research, experimentation and photography skills, she did her level best to find all the great benefits of evaporated milk.

There were many benefits for babies who are unable to drink whole milk. She proved that the fat globulin broke up to make it easier for babies to consume evaporated milk as opposed to regular cow's milk.

Meta struggled to complete her graduate work in 1925-1927. Eventually, she abandoned her studies as the work load at the Milk Association was greater than she can handle. After acquiring two incomplete semesters she finished with her formal education, never to return to college life again as a student. In 1927, she would close the door on the University of Chicago forever.

Torn between her full education and her career was just some of what she felt. She knew women who had Ph.D.'s in the field of home economics. It may have been her dream to complete her education with a doctorate in the field. This aspiration would elude her. She did keep her ties with many of her classmates and other professionals, as we found twenty-five such women who helped her in accomplishing several of her future endeavors.

Her many and varied subjects that she studied brought her much success in her many careers in the future. She studied home economics, experimental cooking, agriculture, scientific management, botany, gardening, organic food chemistry, theories of teaching food and textiles, and many other subjects as documented within her transcripts from the University of Chicago. These subjects would serve her well as she navigated her way through the rest of her life.

Meta Given wrote that she taught grammar school as early as 1902 at the age of fourteen. She may have done this to support herself during her years of education. Meta Given continued teaching according to the Patterson's American Education directory, which documented the teaching lives of many educators throughout the 1900s.

Meta Given started changing careers through her writing articles, which were published in many newspapers from as early as 1925 and continued through 1950. Her first articles may have been based on research she was performing through the University of Chicago during her graduate studies.

Meta Given's 1926 association with the Better Health Bureau while she was performing research at the University of Chicago is not clear. If it was through her education, there was no proof of employment, only a mention in the article at the time.

In a newspaper article from February 05, 1926 written by Meta Given titled "Teaching Girls to Cook," there is a reference to her being associated with the Better Health Bureau. There is no other mention throughout her career of this association in any articles or biography pieces later on.

Meta Given had early associations with the Better Health Bureau, the Canned Milk Association, and the National School of Pressure Cookery in Eau Claire, Wisconsin critiquing pressure-cooking techniques. The only company she may have worked for was the one mentioned as the Evaporated Milk Association.

This information was mentioned in her newspaper articles, as well as a byline in the *Industrial and Engineering Chemistry* journal dated September 1928 (vol. 20. No. 9, page 966). The article is titled *Textures of Ice Creams as Influenced by Some Constituents* by Meta H. Given, Director of the Home Economics Department, Evaporated Milk Association, Chicago, Ill.

And there was mention in the 1930 U.S. Census that she was a dietitian for the Milk Association. This information was probably not from Meta Given; she might say that she was the Director of the Home Economics Department for the Milk Association.

Meta Given's illustrious career as a home economist is just in the infancy as we find her leaving her school days behind from grammar school as early as 1893 until 1927 when she was working towards her masters in home economics.

Meta Given was a humble and hardworking person who learned her craft at the elbow of her parents on a small Ozark farm in Missouri. She did not seek the spotlight; however, they were hers for the taking as the years would pass by and she became one of the most famous home economists of her time. Yet, history would not be as kind to her and her accomplishments as she had been to a nation during two World Wars, the Cold War, even the Korean and Vietnam wars through the 1970s.

By the time the Berlin Wall came down in 1989, Meta Given was all but forgotten as a key player in the American fabric. One person remembered. That was Jane Nickerson, who would continue to write about Meta Given from the interview in 1975 through the mid-1980s. Jane Nickerson wrote a lone memorial newspaper piece to remember a giant upon her passing in 1981.

I am here to right those wrongs and share the rich history of the United States through the life of a valuable and notable home economist, scientist, author, journalist, consultants, entrepreneur, dietician and even food photographer. Welcome Meta Hortense Given back into the main stream of women in history, lest we forget her name, or any of her accomplishments.

LONG LIVE META HORTENSE GIVEN!

# Chapter Four

## Dynamic Duo

## Carrie and Meta from bio articles

*I dedicate this chapter to my dear sister SusieQ.*

META Given's sister Carrie Given was quite a house on fire, similar to her sister Meta. Carrie gets the same education as Meta through Normal school. They attend the same schools growing up. I have found documentation that they both attended the same Normal School #2 in Warrensburg, Missouri, as noted in the catalogue of the State Normal School, Second District of Missouri. A record shows Carrie and Meta Given were in school together and both as "being from Gasconade County."

Carrie was born March 1, 1890 making her Meta's little sister. They seemed to be very close. Not just in the things they did, but in the sharing of life experiences. I find many articles in the *Owensville Republic* newspaper out of Missouri which talked about the many visits they shared over the years with each other.

When I tried contacting the now University of Missouri out of Warrensburg, they had no records of Meta. I was puzzled, thinking that I had the wrong school. When researching through the Alumni, I could not find records of Meta or Carrie. But as I did more research, I discovered that the school had a major fire after Meta left and while she was taking classes at the University of Chicago.

The school burned down, taking most of the records with the school. Once I realized that the records had burned, I abandoned further research.

Carrie taught school for many years. She taught four years, from 1918 to 1922, at the Owensville schools. Then from about 1922 until 1927 she was the principal of the Owensville schools. Carrie also worked on the plays and other entertainment at the school.

Carrie worked on banquets put on by different classes, like the junior class banquet, which included the senior class and alumni. In 1926 after Carrie won the job of principal again for the fourth year in a row, she married in the summer to William J. Aufder Heide.

William had been married before and fought in World War I (The Great War, as it was called then). He and his first wife had two children. The first child died and his wife died soon after having their second son. As a widower, he wanted to marry again, and in 1926 he and Carrie tied the knot.

The article in the Owensville newspaper covered the wedding, as they did in the day. They mentioned both the bride and the groom. Carrie was the principal at their local school and Mr. William J. Aufder Heide owned a dry goods business with his brothers.

The couple surprised their family and friends with their wedding in St. James. It appears that Mr. Aufder Heide picked up his bride at her home in

Bland, Missouri, to be whisked away to their wedding. They married on July 20, 1926, soon after Carrie won another contract to be principal at the Owensville High School for the fourth year in a row.

They would spend several days traveling around Missouri at the following locations for the honeymoon: Steelville, Arcadia, Potosi and Flat River before returning home.

The Aufder Heides were both famous in their little town in Missouri, Owensville. Carrie was the second daughter of Ann Given and James Given of Bland, Missouri who were formerly of Bourbois Township, Missouri of Gasconade County. She was a teacher and then a principal at the Owensville High School for seven years. The principal job was one elected by the school board each year. She was described as "a splendid teacher and worked on the play productions for many years."

Mr. Aufder Heide was a local celebrity of the town, being "one of the most recognized business men of our city, is a partner in the firm of Aufder Heide Bros." The paper placed the information as a way to congratulate the couple and wish them every bit of happiness. They also mentioned that they would be living in the local area of Owensville.

I found it interesting that they wrote, "we trust Mrs. Aufder Heide will continue her work as principal of Owensville High School." At this time, it was common practice to let a married woman go from her job, especially in the school system. Carrie would finish out the 1926-1927 school year as principal.

Their marriage brought them together; however, it ended her full-time career as principal. The following year her contract as principal was not renewed, and she only worked sporadically after her marriage. This was the custom of the day: women could not continue teaching and other professions after they married, or even for some if they were dating.

An article in the *Owensville Republican* newspaper tells all about the opening day of the Owensville schools. It includes the date, which was the 6 of September in 1926. They anticipate the size of the enrollment, which include all grades. They mentioned that Carrie was the principal and taught science, and her degree was obtained for teaching from Warrensburg Normal School.

The Owensville newspaper the *Gasconade* often put pieces in about what was going on with school events. In May 28 of 1926, the Principal Miss Carrie Given and the high school teachers placed a note saying how proud they were of the class of '26 and invited all to join with congratulations and good wishes for their future.

For instance, on the 30 of April in 1926 the newspaper wrote how the junior class entertained the senior class and alumni with a banquet which they believe surpassed many years running in its glory and beauty. The theme was *Alice in Wonderland,* which included decorations reminding one of Snow White with beautiful candles that covered the expanse of the auditorium, with many guest speakers mentioning their esteemed Principal

Miss Carrie Given. Within the report of the evening's events the writer leaves us with sweet remembrance of the magical evening.

Another event orchestrated by Miss Carrie Given was the sophomore class play called *The Adventures of Grandpa*. Noting there have been many plays with better plots, the writer does not think the school ever had a cast of characters so well-rehearsed and a play with such well-developed characters. Laughter reverberated throughout the auditorium, with high marks from all who were present. Miss Carrie Given oversaw the rehearsals, and Miss Given is due much credit for the success of the play.

Miss Carrie Given was very popular in the Owensville and Bland area, as she had several articles written about her over the years. For instance, on January 5, 1926, she entertained the Bland faculty in her mother's home in Bland, Missouri. At 6:30, the guests found their way into the dining room and did ample justice to the three-course dinner. I can imagine it must have been quite good. With the cooking skills of her mother and her famed sister Meta, I am sure Carrie was a chip off the old block.

Yet another snippet in the *Gasconade* newspaper notes that on December of 1926 Mrs. William Aufder Heide was busy preparing for the junior class play performed in January.

In a 1940 bio article about Carrie's sister Meta, it notes Carrie attended the same Teachers College at Warrensburg as her sister. They noted Carrie obtained a degree in science. As we know from earlier articles, she taught the sciences as a school teacher and during her time as the principal. It was often the custom for principals to teach as well as perform the duties of principal.

Carrie (Given) Aufder Heide did not win the principal's position again after her marriage. However, in March of 1943 when the then principal resigned his position, the Board of Education employed Carrie Given-Aufder Heide to the former principal's position for the remainder of the school year. They welcomed Carrie Given-Aufder Heide to their school and were very grateful to her for her assisting in the emergency. She stepped into her former position with ease given her previous experience.

Carrie often kept busy with other projects, such as elections, as noted in the March 18, 1943 *Gasconade Republic,* when she was chosen as an alternate in the election process. Carrie with other people from Owensville took a trip in July of 1938 to go to the opera "Rosalie" at the Municipal Theatre in St. Louis.

Carrie lost her husband August 25, 1961 in Owensville, and he is buried in the Owensville City Cemetery in Owensville, Missouri. He was born the same year as Meta, Carrie's sister. His birthday was November 23, 1888. John had two children, Robert and John, with his first wife Flora Estella Britton (1890-1923).

Meta Given and her mother lived together the rest of their lives, between 1930 and 1949, when Ann, her mother, passed away. Meta and her mother as well as her sister spent time in Florida around the end of the 1940s through 1960s.

Meta had obtained a house in Chicago around the 1930s, where she and her mother lived. There were plenty of rooms, for Meta had two renters in the 1930s, before and during the World's Fair held in Chicago at the time.

Meta Given never learned how to drive, possibly taking the train or local subway, the "L" as it has become known, as her mode of transportation. When Meta Given advertised for renters in the 1930s, she mentions the house had a garage they could use if they drove, there were many boulevards around the house and breakfast was included for an extra amount if they should choose.

At some point in the 1930s, Meta Given offered her garage to friends of her church, as they were without a home for a period. The granddaughter of this family talked about this on the blog *Sandy's Chatter*. It was a heartwarming story indicative of Meta Given's character.

The teller relays her family were the benefactors of not only her garage; the grandfather built a floor out of wood scavenged from torn-down buildings. But they received help from the many types of projects Meta Given was working on at her scientific kitchens.

One of the projects was the testing of clothes detergent. Meta needed clothes to wash, and the family could benefit with freshly laundered clothing for the children, as Meta did this for more than just this family. Another project Meta Given's Scientific

Kitchen worked on was the taking of photographs of foods. Meta distributed the food to families in need, either those staying in her garage or through the church.

It has been noted in a variety of places that Meta Given and her family were Christians, and this story and others shows she not only went to church, but she practiced what she learned by giving of herself to others through the gifts she possessed through her work.

Meta Given spent the years from 1925 until 1948 either working for companies or organizations or her own business. Meta Given gave up her Scientific Kitchen business through encouragement. We found her selling her items in a 1948 ad listing many of her kitchen appliances and gadgets. She continued to live in Chicago, but around 1949 she was in Florida also.

Their mother passed away in Florida, per Ann's obituary in the Bland, Missouri newspaper. Meta placed the obituary in the newspaper. She also saw to it that her mother and father were buried beside each other for all eternity at the Bland, Missouri graveyard. Meta Given remains in the Florida area from about 1949 until the end of her life.

Meta, her sister Carrie, and their mother visit back and forth with each other through the years as documented in the Owensville, Missouri newspaper the *Gasconade Republic*. Either Meta left Chicago to visit her family or they went to Chicago to visit Meta. Here are a few of the articles:

One of the neat things of the time was local newspapers gave the "gossip" of the day in their paper. For instance, they said who was in town from out of town, or they talk about who had been out of town or was going out of town and where they were visiting.

In 1925 during the Christmas holiday, Meta Given traveled home from the Chicago area for a holiday visit with her mother Mrs. James H. Given and her sister Carrie, only to return to Chicago her home after the first of the new year, 1926. Soon after this article came out, Meta Given's article about fudge came out – oh to be a fly on wall when the three of them were talking about what each other was doing during this time.

Meta was going to publish an article. The article was published in many newspapers over the next few years including the *Gasconade County Republican*. Principal Carrie and her teaching adventures included orchestrating various plays by different grade levels in the Owensville High School. It must have been around this time Carrie and William Aufder Heide, started courting as they married in the summer of 1926.

One such snippet in the July 9, 1926 edition of the *Gasconade County Republican* tells of Meta Given coming home for the Fourth of July holiday. At this time, did Carrie confide in Meta she be getting married soon to William, or was it just as much a surprise for Meta as it was for Carrie and William's friends as the article states on the 23rd of July? Oh, to be privy to those conversations at that time.

# MY TIME WITH META GIVEN

As there is no mention of who stood up with Carrie and William when they married, we will probably never know this information. I did see their marriage application. At that time, there was no mention of their witnesses.

Within the pages of the *Gasconade County Republican* we learn that Meta and her mother Ann owned land at the family farm. On March 4, 1927, there was a land notice where Ann and Meta were offered mining leases to land in Red Bird at $1 and royalties.

On June 3, 1927, there was mention of Meta Given accompanied by a Miss Violet Wong and R. H. Shaw from Chicago to visit with Ann Given, Meta's mother. Mr. Shaw was a publicist from the Evaporated Milk Association where Meta Given went to work from 1925 through 1930. Ms. Wong, a Chinese lady, was employed at the Foreign Exchange Department of the Harris Trust and Savings Bank. Meta and Violet hung out for the week while Mr. Shaw then went back at the end of the weekend.

This notice appears in 1927 when Meta and Carrie's mother Ann moved to Chicago with Meta. According to the August 19, 1927 *Gasconade County Republican* newspaper Mr. and Mrs. Wm. J. Aufder Heide and son, John, leave on a Wednesday for Chicago, Illinois, to visit with Mrs. Aufder Heide's sister, Miss Meta Given, and her mother, Mrs. James H. Given. A friend accompanied them as far as St. Louis.

From an October 28, 1927 article in the *Gasconade County Republican* news, we learn Meta Given went to visit her sister Carrie over the weekend, leaving on Monday by way of Cincinnati, Ohio. Meta was leaving Owensville, Missouri to return to her home in Chicago at the end of her visit.

In 1928 there was a real estate transfer between Meta Given and Gasconade Lead Co. for a quitclaim to 80 acres at Red Bird. There were other transfers noted at the same time, but this is the only mention in this article. No mention of any money transferring hands. This type of real estate deed was used to convey property — a formal renunciation or relinquishing of a claim. So, this deed contains no warranties of title at all.

In 1932 Meta Given was found visiting with her sister in June. Meta spent Sunday and Monday with her sister. Meta was in between having finished with the *Chicago Tribune* as their home economics Food Editor having worked on the column "Tribune Food Talk," which was written by Jane Eddington a pen name for Caroline S. Maddocks from 1910 until 1930, when Meta Given took over the column. This column was later written by Mary Meade, a fictional name used by about five authors until the 1970s when the last author, Ruth Ellen Church retired.

Oh, what Meta and Carrie had to talk about! Their careers had been determined for them by others. After being let go from her principal position in 1927, Carrie worked sporadically thereafter. Meta started her home economics career in 1925 only to be let go from not one but two jobs during the early

1930s. There was certainly plenty of fodder for discussion about their careers and what Meta would do next as she was out of a full-time job at the time.

In September of 1937, in a real estate article it is noted Ann gives the State of Missouri the right-of-way for a farm-to-market road from Bland to Red Bird. Ann gave 35-100 acres for the sum of $40 and Meta Given gave 1.2 acres for $75. There were many other pieces of property involved in the making of the farm-to-market road.

In a 1940 bio piece in the Gasconade Country Republican newspaper, tells about Meta and Carrie attended the same *normal school* to obtain their teaching certificates. Meta Given obtained hers in *home economics* and Carried obtained hers in Science. Meta Given attended the Oak Forrest School in Gasconade county, and the first school where she taught grade school was at the Enterprise School in Maries county. At this school, she started teaching at the early age of fourteen. She taught the second grade initially and then she taught at St. James High School. This was once she finished Normal school obtaining her high school teaching certificate.

The only medical problem Meta Given has ever been noted to have had was a heart attack. While an article on July 4, 1940 does not tell why Meta Given was at the hospital, it does tell us her sister travels from Owensville to Chicago to visit with her mother and sister. Miss Given was to be operated on soon and Carrie remained in Chicago to help care for her sister. After Meta Given had her heart attack she tells how she lost weight and remained at the same weight for the rest of her life.

We do find Carrie keeping up her education skills and going back to work to assist the Owensville High School Board of Education to complete the school year as their Principal left in March of the 1943 school year. The article accepts Carrie Given-Aufder Heide with open arms and is very grateful to her for aiding in this emergency. The article mentions Carrie Given had been a teacher at the Owensville schools, but we also know she was a principal for the school for four school years in the 1920s from 1922-1927.

In 1943, an ad ran about the rental of a six-room farmhouse. Ann Given mother of Meta and Carrie still owned the family home, which was about seven miles south of Bland, Missouri. They were offering the house to a factory worker who might like a good garden plot, small orchard with apples and peaches and a wonderful place to raise chickens, with a pasture for a cow.

This property also had a henhouse, garage, and outer buildings. They also noted the farm-to-market road. To make rental arrangements they should contact Carrie Given-Aufder Heide of Owensville, Missouri.

In an additional article right below, they were offering the land that remained of the farm as a pasture for cattle in the spring and summer. There was a well for water, and the price was one dollar per month per head of cattle.

In 1944, there was an article about a club holding a meeting called the Happy Hour Extension Club, which was to give a demonstration called "Favorite Desserts Under Rationing," which had as one of the food leaders Mrs. William (Carrie) Aufder Heide. The interesting thing about this article is it is the first one with a byline – Mrs. Gussie Bade. Very seldom do these articles offer the identity of who may have written them.

In 1945, Meta Given finally sells her share of the family farm. On September 27, 1945, a land transfer between Meta Given and L. C. Cook transfer 80 acres near Red Bird for one dollar. A new chapter started in Meta Given's life. Final ties to her family home were severed with this transfer.

In 1946, there was an announcement in the *Gasconade Country Republican* newspaper to congratulate Miss Carrie Given high school principal and William J. Aufder Heide, a well-known businessman, were married in St. James "20 Years Ago." This was a way to commemorate their many years together. How time flies when you are having fun!

Meta and Carrie did not only meet at each other's home per an article written June 26, 1947, they also met in St. Louis. Mrs. Aufder Heide and some of her friends attend the home economics demonstrations. Carrie and Meta stayed in St. Louis for a while to catch up and enjoy the city. Meta Given had a booth at the exhibition through her business, "Meta Given's Scientific Kitchens." During this time, Meta

Given had just finished her second cookbook called *Meta Given's Encyclopedia of Cooking*.

Meta and her mother start traveling south as early as 1939, as reported in the *Gasconade Country Republican* newspaper. In March, Ann Given and Meta Given of Chicago, Illinois spent the weekend visiting with their daughter and sister, Carrie and her family. From there, they traveled to the South for an extended tour.

In 1947, Carrie continued to travel to Chicago to visit her mother Ann and sister, the very famous Meta Given. The article in the *Gasconade County Republican* did not give any details about their visit, but it was at the height of Meta's career. Her second cookbook was published, and her first cookbook was flying off the shelves and making its way into many universities and colleges around the world.

For years, there were articles about Carrie being an alternate during elections. Finally, in 1947, Carrie and another were appointed as judges of the election. She had finally won a spot as a judge. It only took about twenty years. There is a woman with perseverance and conviction. Also, in 1947 Carrie was a substitute teacher for a Mr. Jackson during his absence while his wife had an operation.

During the long hot days of summer, on August 12, 1948 Carrie and her husband William visited with Carrie's mother, Ann, and her sister, the nationally famous home economist Meta Given in Chicago. They spent two weeks enjoying all the city of Chicago had to offer with their family.

# MY TIME WITH META GIVEN

The unthinkable happened in 1949: the matriarch of the family, Ann Given, died on April 11th at the age of eighty-four while in Florida. Meta, her mother, and Carrie spent time in Florida over the years from the early 1940s through the rest of each of their lives. Their mother was with Meta at Avon Park, Florida. Ann's obituary was listed in *The Bland Courier* out of Bland, Missouri on April 14, 1949. Ann formerly lived on a farm south of Bland, but in more recent years lived in Chicago with her daughter Meta Given, the noted writer.

Ann was survived by her other daughter, Mrs. Wm. J. Aufder Heide of Owensville, Missouri. The body lay in state at the Gottenstroeter Funeral Home of Owensville after Thursday noon. Funeral services for Ann were conducted Friday at 10:30 o'clock from the funeral home with interment in the Bland Union cemetery next to her beloved husband James Henry Given, who died in 1920.

All family gatherings thereafter consisted of Meta and her sister with her sister's husband. The family was pretty small to begin with, but by the 1950s it was even smaller. Meta and her sister were all they had in the world. While they probably still had many aunts, uncles, and cousins, the line of Samuel Given through Carrie and Meta was coming to a close.

During Meta Given's visit around the holidays, they visited with friends in the Salem area. Meta, Carrie and William would take a short ride to Salem for a visit with friends.

In June of 1950, Carrie and Mrs. Aug. Aufder Heide spent Friday in St. Louis. They were accompanied by Miss Meta Given, the famed retired home economist and author of two cookbooks. After the visit, Miss Meta Given returned to her home in Chicago and the Aufder Heide ladies returned to Owensville.

In August of 1950, Meta Given left Chicago for a week to visit her sister Carrie and Carrie's husband Mr. William J. Aufder Heide. On November 30th of 1950, John Aufder Heide, the stepson of Mrs. William J. Aufder Heide went to St. Louis on a Monday. From there, Mrs. Aufder Heide left to go to visit her sister Miss Meta Given of Chicago.

Well into the 1950s, the *Gasconade County Republican* out of Owensville, Missouri was still relaying little bits of information about visits between families. On November 29, 1951, Miss Meta Given of Chicago spent her Thanksgiving holidays with her sister Carrie and Carrie's husband, Mr. William J. Aufder Heide.

The family visits continued in March of 1952, as Mrs. William J. Aufder Heide left on a Tuesday for Chicago, Illinois to visit for two weeks with her sister, Miss Meta Given, the retired home economist and noted author of two very famous cookbooks.

You'd think by now there was more to write about than the family visits of noted families in the area, but we find in September of 1952, Meta Given of Chicago arrived last week to visit with her sister Carrie and Carrie's husband Mr. William Aufder Heide of Owensville.

In 1953, in the late spring of June, Miss Meta Given of Chicago went on Friday to visit for a week with her sister, Carrie and Carrie's husband, Mr. William Aufder Heide. They also arranged to visit with other relatives in the area during Meta's visit.

Miss Meta Given continued to visit with her sister, Carrie and Carrie's husband William Aufder Heide during the early spring of 1955.

The last article I have in my research was about a surprise party for the grandchild of Mr. and Mrs. William Aufder Heide, their son John's daughter. Miss Aufder Heide then left for Los Angeles to spend several weeks with relatives. There was another article that told about Miss Aufder Heide's marriage in 1965.

Before this, William Aufder Heide, Carrie's husband of 35 years, died in August of 1961. His son John and granddaughter survived him, as did his wife Carrie. "In his passing, Owensville loses another of its highly-respected businessmen, one who contributed much toward the growth and development of our fine city." These were the final words of the obituary about William James Aufder Heide.

The years go by, with Carrie and Meta living between Missouri and Florida. We find Carrie Aufder Heide's obituary was listed on November 14, 1970.

Mrs. Carrie Aufder Heide, age eighty, 375 South School Ave., Sarasota, died Friday at Sarasota Memorial Hospital. She moved to Sarasota two years ago from Owensville, Missouri. She was a retired school teacher, (principal) and also a member of Church of Christ in Osprey.

She left a stepson, John W. Aufder Heide, Owensville, Mo. and a sister Meta Given, Sarasota, Florida.

Funeral services would be held at Roberts Funeral Home, Inc., S. Links Avenue at Ringling Boulevard, in Missouri, on Monday at ten A.M., conducted by Don Hastings. Friends may call Sunday at two to four and seven to nine p.m. The family requests flowers be omitted and those who wish may make contributions to the heart fund. (Indicating she may have died of a heart attack.)

Several pieces of information exist regarding the family, such as where she lived in Sarasota, and the church she and possibly her sister attended in Sarasota. The address appears to have been changed over years.

Meta Given's family seemed to have some longevity as her mother was born in 1866 and lives to be eighty-three years old, dying in 1949. Her father did not live quite as long, as he was born in 1858 and died in 1920 at the age of sixty-two. Still about fifteen years longer than the life expectancy of the time. Meta's paternal grandparents Charity and Henry lived to be eighty and seventy-seven, respectively. Life expectancy at the time was around forty years of age, so, they all lived well past the average life expectancy.

Family is where you have your first friends, your first lessons of life. Family is where you learn to cook, plant a garden, harvest a crop and preserve the bounty. At least at the turn of the twentieth century, these were the ways many people lived their lives.

The country was founded on hearty stock, such as people who cared for their family, and people who believed there was nothing wrong with demanding work.

Family was everything. Each person in the family had their place. Each person had their individual chores, but they could all come together to complete a major project like bringing in the harvest, raising a barn or delivering a baby.

Children worked at a young age. They provided extra hands, took care of younger siblings, planted gardens, and learned to cook before the age of ten. They possibly were concocting their own recipes or working on other projects on their own.

Parents had many children, usually to increase the workforce for the farm or business. Also, mortality rates for children and wives were high. So, it was not uncommon to have many children. If a wife died in childbirth or of some other disease, then the husband often re-married.

This was the case in both Meta and Carrie Given's lives, since Meta learned to cook at a young age and Carrie became the wife of a widower with a young son, probably someone she met when she taught school for many years before marrying. Both women started working at a young age and became school teachers.

At the time of writing this biography, there is no one left to talk to about Meta and Carrie Given. In

1922, when Meta stopped teaching, a student she taught could be about 107 years old today. Someone she worked with might be in their eighties or nineties. I tried following a few paths, but each person had passed away. For instance, Jane Nickerson the food editor has passed away.

Her mother, father and sister are all gone. Her brother-in-law is gone and her step-nephew has passed away as well.

The publishing company for her books has been swallowed up by another company, Doubleday. I acquired her college transcript, but there is no one there who remotely remembered her. They were hesitant to give up her transcript; however, I was able to convince them there was no one in the family to inquire about her.

I tried to obtain her death certificate, but because I am not a family member, I could not obtain it. However, there were thousands of articles and some biography pieces about Meta on the Internet and there were colleges willing to help where they could.

Meta Given had many articles written about her by various columnists. For instance, on April 14, 1942, Francis C. Walker wrote a very nice piece about Meta Given, who was directing demonstrations at Gimbel Victory Cooking School.

The most personal information about Meta Given was within her own articles. As she wrote about food, she told about how much she loved food, and how she was influenced by her dad and mom regarding her love of food and its preparation. She talks passionately about muffins, apples, and beets.

There is not much mention about any health issues for either Carrie or Meta. However, Meta Given does mention later in life she did have a heart attack which helped her to decide to slow down. The 1975 article written by Jane Nickerson mentions the incident but does not give us any real details as to when or what around the actual event. Also, there was mention of Meta Given being in the hospital in 1940, but no details for the reason.

By piecing this article and the 1975 article I conclude she may have had the heart attack in 1940, not around 1948 as it eludes to in the 1975 article. As you will find there are some details a little different with this 1940 article and the 1975 article mentioned in more detail in this book.

Many times, I have found the details of Meta's life may be a little different from various articles, information in her books and other places used for fact checking like the new wiki page, initially published in 2014.

To have an actual interview with Meta Given in her eighties must have been amazing. I know why Jane Nickerson sought out Meta Given – admiration. Think of the history that lay within Meta Given. She had spent eighty-some years by living. She was a brave woman who had been taught by her parents to be an entrepreneur through their work on the farm. Many people think farming has nothing to do with being an entrepreneur, but many an entrepreneur started their life doing just as Meta had done: working hard on their family farm.

Each one of these articles brings to life the amazing story of Meta Given, Carrie Given, Ann Given, James Given, John Given, Henry Given, William Given and so on, going back all the way to Hugh Given. Their lives were something really special. Each one of them contributed just a little to Meta's over all being. Each one passed a little of themselves on to the next generation. In their stories, their teaching and their living. This little piece made up a whole person Meta Given.

Meta Given grew into an amazing woman who taught, wrote, investigated, photographed, and cooked her way through the American fabric for all people as their very own home economist, dietitian, food editor, journalist and eventually she would feed a nation with the most nutritious food at the best economy. We need Meta Given today as much as we needed her during World War II. People complain about the very thing Meta Given did then, which is providing their families with a nutritious, economical meal.

What a woman Meta Given was. Many people have said her cookbooks are dated and antiquated; one person even said you should never use her instruction in canning in her cookbooks. Funny thing is, there are still millions of people who are using her recipes today. What is old is new again. I know my family still uses her recipes as we did sixty years ago, when my mother purchased her copy of *Meta Given's Modern Encyclopedia of Cooking* cookbook in the early 1950s.

# MY TIME WITH META GIVEN

If they are antiquated, so be it. I prefer eating a nutritious meal from an antiquated, outdated recipe than some newfangled recipe that is not worth the paper (or Internet resource) it is printed on or hard drive that holds it. Show me a nutritious meal that is economical, and I'll show you a Meta Given classic recipe that will win, hands down. I wonder if Bobby Flay would take on one of her recipes in the *"throw down."*

Not sure what operation Meta had, as referenced in this article "1940-07 (Jul) – Wm. J. Aufder Heide received word this week Miss Meta Given was operated on in Chicago, Illinois on Saturday and was getting along as well as could be expected. Mrs. Aufder Heide is in Chicago staying with her mother, Mrs. Ann Given, and her sister, Miss Given." As you can see, Meta's sister had a great devotion for Meta and mother. She never let them go through any crisis alone—she was right there, even though she had her own family by this time.

I can imagine it was a sad day for the Given women to let go of their family farm. While no one had lived there for years, since they were renting the farmhouse and land for years, it is still a sad day when the transfer occurs. They had to say goodbye to the farm, goodbye to the good old days, goodbye to all they held dear.

Today with findagrave.com, it makes it easier than ever to locate a loved one in their final resting place. I have located where Meta Given's parents' final resting place is at the Bland Union Cemetery. With time and luck, I have been able to locate Meta

Given's final resting place in Sarasota, Florida. Her death certificate still eludes me as I am not a member of her family.

I noticed there were several days missing in the *Lakeland Ledger* newspaper online. After careful research, I noticed there was more than one day per listing. Therefore, the dates which were missing are tagged on an earlier day. This is how I found her obituary.

By the mid-1950s, the articles about Meta Given and her sister Carrie (Mrs. William Aufder Heide) die out. However, William Aufder Heide's son John Aufder Heide was in the news over the years about his schooling. Then in the 1960s there are several articles about John's daughter.

I found the marriage announcement of Carrie and Meta's parents listed "1887-03 (Mar) 25 Eliza A(nn) Lacy married James H. Given(s) in book 1 page 365 officiant J. J. Burns, J. P. both of Leduc, Gasconade County, Missouri."

The intimate lives of the Given women were often posted in the *Gasconade Republican* newspaper. That was how it was done in the era. People were interested in the people of the town. The newspaper was happy to oblige, and the townspeople were happy to contribute. Without these intimate stories, short and sweet as they are, we might not know little details about the goings-on of Meta and Carrie Given, the Aufder Heide family and their mother Ann Given.

The one newspaper article eluding me was the obituary of Meta Given. She died on November 17,

1981 at the age of 93 and three-quarters. She was living in Lakeland, Florida at the time. Her sister died about eleven years prior in Sarasota, Florida.

You might think for such a famous person as Meta Given, there should have been many obituaries or memorial pieces in every newspaper her column ran, but alas, it was not to be Meta Given's fate at the end of her life. No one really seemed to be interested in Meta Given any longer.

There was one memorial piece placed in the *Lakeland Ledger* newspaper by Jane Nickerson who had interviewed Meta Given for the last time in 1975. She was kind enough to do a memorial piece of Meta after reading about her obituary in the same newspaper. Jane wrote for the *Lakeland Ledger* in the 1980s. Jane had switched papers sometime between the late 1970s and early 1980s.

Meta's life began with a bang, with two very remarkable snowstorms in 1888, but her passing almost went unremarked except for Jane Nickerson's article.

Meta Given passed away on November 17, 1981 at the Presbyterian Nursing Home. A native of Missouri, she moved to Lakeland, Florida from Sarasota, Florida seven years prior. She was a retired school teacher, a former cooking writer for the *Chicago Daily Sun* and a member of the Church of Christ and the National Association of Retired Persons.

Meta's cousin Thomas Enoch Farrell of Springfield, Missouri is the only surviving relative listed in her obituary. Under funeral services in the same paper, it has some of the same listed information with the time, who officiated and her final resting place at the Sarasota Memorial Park Cemetery in Sarasota, Florida.

# Chapter Five

## The Cookbook

*I dedicate this chapter to my daughter Laurel Mondou*

COOKBOOKS were written in the colonies originally by individuals for passing down recipes (receipts) in the family and keepsakes. A self-proclaimed orphan Amelia Simmons wrote the first known published cookbook using local products. She was a domestic in the late 1700s. Often the domestics were not very well educated. Their education was through "hard knocks." Amelia was just such a person.

She learned her trade by doing, as she was an orphan. The only hope for a woman was the kindness of others. They would take you in, expect you to work for little or no money, and the only education imparted was by doing the job. The reading and writing and other educational pursuits were not considered important.

Amelia's cookbook was called *American Cookery, or the art of dressing viands, fish, poultry, and vegetables, and the best modes of making pastes, puffs, pies, tarts, puddings, custards, and preserves, and all kinds of cakes, from the imperial plum to plain cake*: Adapted to this country, and all grades of life. (Hartford: Printed for Simeon Butler, Northampton, 1798). This book was published about 100 years before Meta Given was born.

Amelia was not only a self-proclaimed orphan, she was also illiterate. Yet she had the fortitude to not only learn her craft, but to want to pass on what she knew. Obviously, she had truly learned the hard way. She did not want anyone else to go through what she had gone through. Hence, her legacy, the wonderful *American Cookery* cookbook.

There were many other cookbooks written between that time (1798) and when Meta Given wrote her second cookbook, about 150 years later, in 1942. Amelia's cookbook started the revolution of cookbooks written in the colonies. She was but one of thousands of others over the years. But Amelia stands out amongst them all, as she had very little, yet she was able to put her thoughts together to dictate her book to another and have it published several times. Amelia Simmons's cookbook is available for your viewing at a website online (Alice Ross, 2017).

The Michigan State University did a wonderful project called "Feeding America," which culminated in preserving online early digitized cookbooks. You can find Amelia's, Fannie Farmer's, and even Harriet Beecher Stowe and her sister Catherine's cookbooks. These are some of the most important cookbooks of the nineteenth and twentieth centuries. This collection includes seventy-six of the most important. The project was supported by a grant that took a two-year journey to complete.

These early cookbooks provided the housewife and domestics with the ability to cook meals with recipes, as well as take care of medical emergencies. Cookbooks got a real boost from the growth of the home economics movement, which started around the end of the nineteenth century through much of the twentieth century. Many of these books were written by women, making this a dominated female career.

Another movement that brought about a great influx of change in cookbooks was cooking schools, such as The Boston Cooking School in which Fannie Farmer's *The Boston Cooking-School Cook Book*, published by Boston: Little, Brown and Co., in 1896 was born. Meta Given also provided her own cooking school out of her small business "Meta Given's Scientific Kitchens" out of Chicago, Illinois in the 1930s and 1940s.

Fannie's cookbook brought professionalism and scientific knowledge about nutritional ingredients, dietary needs, and measurement of ingredients, quality and quantities of ingredients. As a matter of fact, Fannie Farmer is credited with being the first to write a cookbook that standardized specific measurements of food, where a cup used a specific measuring cup, instead of the cup of your choice, like tea or coffee possibly.

A great new technological change was afoot that assisted in Fannie's style from the mid-1800s to the early 1900s, with the use of electricity and gas stoves. They replaced the hearths that were being used for everyday cooking and heating. These innovations were responsible for cutting the time and back-breaking labor required to prepare the daily meals. Stoves were made from cast iron starting in the mid-1800s.

Utensils went from being a specialty handmade order by the local blacksmith to being stamped out automatically by machine. These standard items allowed recipes to be uniformly made because everyone could purchase the same items. This changeover in the mid-1800s allowed Fannie Farmer to be more scientific about the measurement of items, thus the revolution of her cooking methodology.

There are lovely pictures of just such utensils on the same Michigan website that houses the early 18-twentieth century cookbooks. Cooking implements can be found at the same website (Alice Ross, 2017).

These inventions changed the cookbook, the kitchen and where people dined ultimately. The room with the hearth was where everyone gathered to eat their meals and socialize. This was often the warmest room in the house, and many times the only room with heat.

With the invention of stoves, electricity, and other conveniences, you no longer needed to eat your dinner in the kitchen. You could have a separate room specially set aside for eating: the dining room. Many times, you find a home that was built before the turn of the twentieth century will have hidden hearths behind false walls, a hidden treasure waiting to be discovered.

With these modern inventions, you could heat multiple rooms in the house with less effort and expense. For instance, my great grandparents had a house with a large circular room as the parlor, with all other rooms leading from there, as the parlor was the only room with heat.

Many new utensils and appliances were invented for the kitchen. There were those that believed these gadgets made the work easier, but in truth, only a few of them made life easier; most of the utensils were unnecessary. But who doesn't love their gadgets?

I have read where people thought Meta Given's recipes required too many utensils. I suppose cooking in general might be considered unnecessary by many, as fewer and fewer people cook over the ages. But to make something really good, you should consider giving it your all, and if it requires a few utensils then so be it. When I make Meta Given's biscuits, I use about six different utensils, that includes the pie plate and the mixing bowl. However, if I had to, I could cut that back to about three or four.

You could use less and I have, depending on what I have at hand. But I find Meta Given's recipes are just dying for her never-ending belief in substitutions. So, if you felt confined by her recipes, it was a confinement you placed on the recipe and its utensils yourself.

There have been a great many cookbooks written over the years. Some so thick that you need a stand to hold the book, others so small and thin you could put it in your pocket. There are all kinds of purposes for cookbooks. Some cover specific ethnic types of cooking: Italian, Chinese, and the like. There are cookbooks that only cover baking or meats.

Then there are cookbooks that try to cover the basics with many favorite recipes, like *Betty Crocker* and *Better Homes and Gardens,* and then there are the cookbooks that are encyclopedias that cover just about everything you can think of: Fannie Farmer, the *Joy of Cooking,* and Meta Given's *Encyclopedia* are just a few that try to cover all things in cookery.

These days, there are many interesting things going on in the world of cookbooks. For instance, Radcliffe College at Harvard University (Chakrabarti, 2017) has a special collection of cookbooks, and University of Minnesota has a website about cooking over the ages.

I have been very fortunate to have had access to these websites to discover all the enthralling things that people are trying to do to preserve the cookbooks of yesteryear and document the cultural changes that have occurred. These changes occurred because of the progression that cookbooks have taken and contributed to over the years (Chakrabarti, Old Cookbooks Find A Home At Harvard, 2017).

Cookbooks have changed over time, and our culture has changed because of or by them. One has aided the other over the years. It is hard to say specifically if the chicken came before the egg—if the cookbook created the standardization of cooking or if cooking standardized the cookbook.

If you look at history, the standardization of utensils came about in the mid- to late 1800s and the first standardized cookbook *The Boston Cooking-School Cook Book* by Fannie Farmer came out in 1896.

So, one could surmise that Fannie took advantage of the latest standardized inventions and utilized the home economic practices of the day to create a cookbook that provided instruction on how to use the newly invented standardized utensils.

The *Joy of Cooking* cookbook was born from a woman who became a widow and needed a way to make money after her husband passed away. She had been someone who collected recipes over the years from parties at her home.

It seemed like a natural progression that she should create a cookbook that she published herself in the first printing in 1931. She was not only author, but marketer and distributor, as well as publisher and editor, which she did out of her humble apartment.

Betty Crocker was not a person but the last name of the Crocker family and a woman's first name that was considered pleasing. These cookbooks are basic and useful cookbooks that show a simple cooking style.

They give general information and are loaded with recipes easy to make in a short period of time. They provide many straightforward recipes for everyday foods that one cooks for their family, often with limited time and resources.

Meta Given's cookbooks, like many others, were intended for the average housewife with menus for every day of the week as well as special occasions. But Meta's books were also written as textbooks, and they were used as such in many universities and colleges in this nation and throughout the world.

Meta's books provided information about food. These books tell you about practically every aspect of food, including the seasons of food. You would be hard-pressed to find the information accumulated in Meta's cookbooks in many other cookbooks collectively.

Meta's cookbooks give you detailed information about nutrition, diet, and the differences of foods, grades of ingredients and how to or when to use one ingredient with another. Meta goes into great depth about cakes, breads, flours, apples, meats, eggs, and so many necessary details about cooking, as well as the kitchen and utensils. As a testament to their longevity, many universities still have her cookbooks on their shelves as reference material.

Meta Given's *Modern Family Cookbook* and *Modern Encyclopedia of Cooking* are scientific endeavors that were overlooked by many for their importance in the history of food and books about home economics. Meta Given the scientist is left out of so many important books, articles and so on.

Reading the book *Rethinking Home Economics* by Sarah Stage 1997, I discovered there was not even one mention of Meta Given. When reading the article in the *Chicago Tribune* by Kristin Eddy 1997 called *Serving Food News For 150 Years*, there was no mention of Meta who wrote the *Tribune Cook Book* and *Food Talk* for one year.

Meta not only provided the how, but the why, the when and the where on food. If you read her books carefully, you will get an extensive education about food. This education would require several courses at a university to cover as much material.

Today you could use these books as historical information about how we got here from before in the dark ages of food understanding from the early twentieth century. You could also use them as a resource to help you get back in touch with food and cooking in the present day.

Meta Given did not write the first cookbook, but she did write an important cookbook that was used as a textbook, reference manual and a cooking manual for the everyday cook/chef. While the terminology in her books may seem antiquated today, you can interchange the word housewife with chef, cook, or primary caregiver, to name a few. These books are just as relevant today as they were over 70 years ago when they were first published. My family has been canning and using this cookbook since the early 1950s without finding this book out-of-date, but instead timeless.

As a reference manual, it is a great sounding board for the basic information about raw ingredients. Some of the information may seem outdated, but it can be used as a reference to find information you may not find as easily anywhere else.

One of the things I like to do is use it as one of my many references. Like researching a paper or a book, you find one reference is just not enough. And using references from different time periods gives you the full picture instead of a narrow perspective of a subject.

In 1947, the North Dakota *Spectrum* placed a feature that their Phi Upsilon Omicron was sponsoring the sale of Meta Given's *Modern Family Cookbook*. They claimed this book was currently being used at the NDAC home economics department as a reference manual. This book was used widely throughout the college and university experience in their home economics and other departments in the 1940. There are well over 200 books still housed in universities throughout this country and many foreign schools as well (Phi U Apron Sale, Special, 1947).

In researching this book, I tried to find information from the period when Meta was growing up as well as information of the current times. Perspectives have changed over the years regarding different subjects. It is nice to see and put the pieces together to come up with the whole picture. For instance, home economics was a very hot subject and career around the turn of the twentieth century, but that subject has become dead by the turn of the twenty-first century. What killed its popularity? Good question.

Who wrote the best cookbook ever? I guess we have more questions than answers, or so it seems. For there are always questions that are difficult to answer. Why, you may ask? Because there are so many great cookbooks and the best cookbook is in the hand of the user and the eye of the beholder.

# MY TIME WITH META GIVEN 77

There are so many great cookbooks. When I read these old classics, I think each one of them must have been the favorite of the day. While I was growing up, the best cookbook was *Meta Given's Encyclopedia of Cooking*. My mother always referred to it as "Meta Given." When I told her others called it their "Bible," she thought that was a fitting reference.

Meta Given's cookbooks are the favorites of many people, according to a survey taken by Abes.com, where 500 readers choose the *Encyclopedia* as number eight. Pretty good for something that has been out of print now for over forty years.

Some people never forget a good cookbook. There are all the beloved recipes that have been passed down from generation to generation and having the "original" cookbook with the recipes, with the torn pages, the flour or chocolate spattered across the recipes with the journal items written between the pages; well, there is nothing quite like that.

My sister handed me our mother's original 1953 Meta Given *Encyclopedia* for Christmas in 2014. I know it was a great sacrifice for her to pass on "Hortense's" work of art that our mother used from the year she (my sister) was born until now. But she handed it to me for safekeeping and for me to pass along all the goodies inside to other family members.

Meta Given has been a household name in our home from the time I was very little. Today she has become my friend through my research of her life. I try to guess things about her life only to find that I uncover yet another fact, like she is baiting me to find all the facts of her life.

When I thought her middle name was Henrietta, she never let me rest until I discovered that it was Hortense. My sister loved the name so much that is how she references Meta now, with a giggle, because it is fun.

As I read the cookbooks of the past, I wonder what cookbooks Meta Given owned, read, and cherished. In one of her newspaper articles she mentions that she had just purchased a bunch of cookbooks for reference in her search for the best recipe, the best technique and to find out what everybody else was doing.

Did she own some of the older cookbooks? Did her mother, grandmother or aunts own cookbooks, and did they bring them with them from Ireland, or from West Virginia? What are the answers to the questions that I have? Will I ever learn everything there is to know about Meta? I am sure I will not.

There is no one left to talk to and answer the questions of the moment. I can only rely on the written word that has been left behind in newspapers, journals and her cookbooks.

As I am writing this, I have found yet another piece of information that is relative to this chapter. I questioned where Meta and her family may have gotten their recipes. Well in 1941, Meta started writing articles for the *St. Louis Dispatch*. They wrote a lovely article about Meta and her first solo meal at the age of nine. She got her recipe from a periodical called *Journal of Agriculture's* cookbook.

This periodical sent cookbooks to their patrons. Meta's first meal included a plain, sweet, yellow cake recipe from this cookbook. We now know of at least one cookbook that Meta Given had in her possession as a young girl.

So far, I have been lucky to find several references for each of the facts that I have uncovered about our Meta Hortense Given. I know where she lived, who her parents were, who was her sister and about their educations. These are just some of those questions that have been answered.

Cookbooks were one of her passions. She did not publish her first official cookbook until 1942. That does not mean that she could not have written it earlier; it appears that she was doing plenty of writing.

She did work on a cookbook project for a publishing company which had her referenced as the authority who revised and enlarged the cookbook in 1936-37. She was associated with the cookbook from 1932-1939. Meta Given was the copyright holder of the book as late as 1939. However, her name was taken off from the title page. Yet another curious question: Why?

She also wrote many pamphlets and books about all kinds of subjects. While she had her business, she decided to keep her staff busy by writing her own cookbook. She had compiled many recipes and articles about all kinds of things regarding cooking, food, nutrition, diet, the kitchen, utensils and all equipment relating to cooking food. Why not compile it into a cookbook?

Heck, it seemed like she had so much material, why not write a second cookbook? Both books were wildly popular, with her selling around three to four million copies over her cookbooks' lifetimes, from 1942-1972.

Did Meta Given truly write "the latest thing in cookbooks," as was told at the time? Did she write something that was never written before? Or was she just bold enough to take information from the past, mix it around and come up with a fresh-looking item that was all the rage, because she was the "go-to-girl" at the time? I'll leave that to your imagination. They certainly contain plenty of information and you will be hard-pressed to find the same information and detail in another cookbook of her time, or any other time for that matter.

Cookbooks are fascinating. There aren't many people who don't own at least one cookbook. I didn't own one until my mother bought me the *Joy of Cooking* cookbook. I really didn't have much use for it. I had learned to cook by watching her cook and obtaining her instruction through that observation. I guess I used a cookbook a few times when I was a kid. My brother Will and I used one to make pizza from the *Betty Crocker* cookbook that used baking powder instead of yeast in the dough. And I also made the best brownies from that cookbook as well.

But other than that, I just "wing" it when I cook. If I wanted something to eat, I just get the ingredients and made it. I watched my mother for twenty years, who needs a cookbook? True: I didn't make bread or that kind of stuff, but somehow, I was able to cook for myself and friends without much effort.

When I tried to use the *Joy of Cooking*, it was confusing and seemed like you had to search all over the cookbook just to complete one recipe. One recipe may be made from three other recipes; I really could not get the hang of that type of reference.

Then someone told me I should treat the *Joy* like a novel. Read the whole thing, and then once you have read it, the recipes will make sense. Sure enough, that worked better than just picking out one recipe. You learn a lot from a cookbook that is well written and gives you extra information about food in general.

For instance, they talk about flour. I didn't know there were so many types of flour and so many different uses. How about eggs and all the things you can do with eggs, like substitutes? I have read about eggs in Meta's cookbooks – just about everything you need to know about eggs can be found between the pages.

I am not sure if I can say the same about other cookbooks. They may provide history. They often provide a snapshot into the past. They provide information about all kinds of things. Each person brings their own self into the book in ways one could not believe. Reading the books from the eighteenth, nineteenth and twentieth centuries is so entertaining.

You never know what someone is going to write about or say about a subject. The raspberry chapter in one of the cookbooks was not at all what I expected. I say, the doctor loved his raspberries and probably had an orgasmic event every time he popped one into his mouth and the flavor burst as he crunched down for the very first time.

Many people have this incredible love of food. You can tell it in their writing on the subject. Meta Given had an unbelievable love of food. She said she got that love of food from her father. Probably, it meant more to her that she could share that love with others especially after he had passed away. I find this to be a neat way for her to be close to him every day through their mutual love - food.

She talked about how food burst in your mouth, how things looked so appealing to the eye, how steam rose up from food and permeated the room and how everyone should find ways to keep food interesting, appealing and fresh.

She could write a dozen recipes for the same dish or make the food into a dozen different dishes. It is so fascinating reading her articles and comparing them to her cookbook recipes. How similar or different they all could be.

But she was not any different from her predecessors. After all there is this one who wrote about 100 different dishes for beef, or lamb or pork. Talk about loving something enough to make the same thing yet reinventing it in so many different techniques.

Meta Given believed that the cookbook should be informative, should be basic, and should be organized. So, did many of the other authors. But everyone has their own idea on these subjects. How entertaining to read each cookbook, not as a cookbook but as a novel.

You can see little glimpses into the lives of each person who wrote their cookbook. The things that they were passionate about revealed their lifestyle: temperance, recipes either of alcohol or using alcohol, good manners, ways to treat your guests, how best to cook this or that and always lecturing about what not to do.

Many people write their books to help others who were just like them: orphans, domestic help, women who needed guidance, men who wanted to help others. Many cookbook authors had to pay for their own publishing. This enabled them to own their books outright, and when additional publishing occurred, they made much of the money themselves.

Hundreds of cookbooks are now published every year. The amazing thing is that fewer people are cooking than ever before. There is this epidemic of purchasing items without actually using them. Cookbooks are just one of the many items.

According to the statista.com web page there have been no less than 2000 cookbooks published since 2003. In 2012 and predicted for 2013 there were over 3000 books sold in those years (2018 statista.com).

If you look at my mother's cookbook, you can tell she used, reused and overused that cookbook. The binding has been taped, the pages are torn out, and the binding groupings are separating from each other. It is a book that was used almost every day from 1953 until 2004 for over fifty years.

I can't say I ever used a cookbook nearly as much. And if you had anything that my mother made, you'd say she was a master chef. She provided more than just the average meal at our table. We ate like kings and queens on a budget that was the envy of "Jack Benny" (a guy known to be conservative with his money, aka "cheap"). Meta Given would have been proud of my mother for the way she budgeted her money, but not at the expense of her family's nutritional needs.

She was able to cook a meal for seven people that included dessert using all of the tricks that Meta Given suggested and so much more. She purchased day-old bread that was cooked that day. She went later in the day after all day-old bread was sold out and bought the bread at the end of the day which was freshly made that day.

After all, back in the '50s and '60s, it was more important to ensure that the less fortunate were taken care of. An empty shelf is not the way you want your customers to perceive you. Today they would not even consider that a problem.

Meta Given had all kinds of tips for the homemaker of the day. At that time, the cook was generally considered to be a woman. Today it could be just about anyone. Homemakers work outside of the home, but that does not make them any less of a homemaker.

Now it is believed that the very first cookbook that was written in English was in 1390. It is claimed that there is no first cookbook written, as the Babylonians, Egyptians, Greeks and even the

Romans had cookbooks for their male cooks of their upper-class households.

Research is a funny thing; sometimes you can start at the beginning, sometimes you begin at the end. But the result remains the same. It is all a collection of information. I am just happy that I was able to find the reference at the beginning of cookbook history, even though finding the first cookbook is probably not going to happen in this research effort.

The first known cookbook to be published in the colonies was in 1742, some 200 years prior to Meta Given's *Modern Family Cookbook*. Meta Given's book was the culmination of her scientific knowledge, the knowledge of her mother, and the many generations that came before. Meta Given used cookbooks and recipes from the past, but tested every recipe, perfected every recipe and made them her very own. Many of her recipes have a 200-year history connected to them.

This cookbook called **The Compleat Housewife: or accomplished Gentlewoman's Companion** was published in 1742 and a wildly popular book by Eliza Smith. The first version of her cookbook was originally published in 1727 in London and then republished in the Colonies. Eliza worked in service, but she had eighteen publishings of her cookbook many after her death.

This cookbook was mentioned by William Carew Hazlitt (22 August 1834 – 8 September 1913) who was an English lawyer, bibliographer, editor and writer of *Old Cookery Books and Ancient Cuisine*

(Hazlitt, 1886), which can be found at Gutenberg online eBooks. He allocated some fifty-four pages specifically to this cookbook in 1893.

He compiled a history of cookery books that included the *Compleat Housewife*, commenting that "the highly curious contents of E. Smith ... may be securely taken to exhibit the state of knowledge in England upon this subject in the last quarter of the seventeenth and the first quarter of the eighteenth century."

Also, in the publishing of *The Compleat Housewife* by William Parks, he used the fifth edition of the original cookbook which was published by him in Williamsburg, Virginia. He deleted recipes he deemed unnecessary because the food stuffs were not available in the colonies, claiming, "the ingredients or materials for which are not to be had in this country."

It took another fifty years before Amelia Simmons, an indentured servant and a self-proclaimed orphan, published the first American cookbook on American Cookery. She heavily borrowed from other authors who were British, specifically from Susannah Carter. However, it is noted that "revolutionary and original aspects of her work lie in its recognition and use of truly American produce."

Cornmeal was as American as produce got from the Indians, which was used to create Indian pudding, Johnny cake and Indian slapjacks. We also find corncob used to smoke bacon and cranberry sauce to accompany another very American dish, roasted turkey, all indigenous to the Americas. An innovation from the new world was pearlash, a leavening for doughs like biscuits, Johnny cake, slapjacks and other breads, which led to today's famous ingredient that we call baking powder.

We not only had the American Revolution in 1776, but we had the first revolution in the modern world of cookery in the United States from 1786-1886. Amelia Simmons's book kicked off the cookery revolution. By the way, she could neither read nor write. So, the next time you say you can't do something – think about Amelia and say – "How can I get this done?"

I found this information thanks to the Feeding America project on the Michigan State University's website. It's an amazing thing, the Internet, as you can find whole copies of original cookbooks untouched as they were at the time they were printed. These cookbooks are fascinating reads, and I encourage anyone interested in learning about these treasures to take a look. They are not only mesmerizing, but a very rich and important part of our history. (MSU, 2003)

After Amelia's cookbook, which had dozens of reprints even some plagiarized whole and in part for the next forty years, we had two factions of cookbooks – the English publishing their cookbooks with special chapters to entice their American audience. The second faction that was really taking off was American authors writing for themselves. These books captured the American public like none other. We were off and running, and let me tell you, the floodgates were open.

Our first black American cookbook was written by Robert Roberts, employed by Christopher Gore, a governor and Senator in Massachusetts. Roberts wrote the *Household Servant's Directory* in 1827 out of Boston.

The book tells none other than how to manage as expected the top ten percent of the day's households in New England. Robert's cookbook revolutionized the status of servants to caterers, concierges and managers of large households in Northern cities like Philadelphia, New York and Boston. These were the only locations the book has been found.

Cookbooks were arranged by authors as they put them together in an organized fashion based upon their imagination. A method that Meta used in her books was to alphabetize, which was first used by Mrs. N. K. M. Lee in *The Cook's Own Book* (Boston, 1832) as an encyclopedia 100 year prior to Meta's first cookbook.

Many of the cookbooks in the 1830s and 1840s gave us the themes that we live with today. You may recognize some of them: "economy and frugality, management and organization, a preoccupation with baking, sweets and desserts, vegetarianism, diet and temperance."

So, Meta Given was not ahead of her time, she was just trying to reiterate what should be obvious but for some reason is worth repeating over and over again. You can eat economically using the highest nutrition if you just keep organized in the management of your household.

Therefore, this trend began in the 1840s, some 100 years before our Meta published her first cookbook.

The increasing number of cookbooks started with one little old book by Amelia Simmons, and there is no end in the foreseeable future. This new career was dominated by women by the mid-nineteenth century. It wasn't until the last quarter of the twentieth century that men increased their numbers in the field.

As a matter of fact, men now act like it's their job, like they invented cookery and women should get out of the kitchen. Women don't let anyone take your jobs or push you out of a field you have dominated for the better part of two centuries.

There was a decline in book publishing, starting around the Civil War, but by 1870 that changed when charitable organizations run by women published cookbooks to help the orphans and families devastated by the Civil War and other good causes, leading us into the twentieth century. We are still practicing this type of charity.

The early cookbooks such as Amelia's missed trivial things like the temperature at which to cook an item or the standardized measurement of one or all of the items. It is possible that there was an assumption about those things by everyone. After all, they were providing information, surely you must come with some foreknowledge. I know when I am writing my technical manuals at work, I do not put in every single detail. I assume the reader has what I consider "given" knowledge.

These cookbooks of the day not only contain recipes and information about cooking. The author may have had an agenda that was not solely food-oriented, but about one's duties as a wife, religion, even assumptions about etiquette in or out of the home.

Then in the late 1800s, the cooking and household arts took on a scientific tone, which became a new field called *home economics*, where cooking became none other than a domestic science. One of our most famous of cookbook authors, teacher and graduate of the Boston Cooking School, Fannie Farmer, was the first to use instructions that were "exact."

Yet another revolution going on was where we went from households ordering their measuring cups and such from the local tin shop or blacksmith to being manufactured uniformly. This consistency created the ability to scientifically manufacture recipes with uncanny accuracy. One cup was the same universally, instead of cooks using their own form of a measuring "tea" cup.

Before this revolution, you fashioned your own recipes that worked for you and seldom worked for anyone else. Even though people complain of the same thing now as then: "when passing on a recipe, it cannot be made the same as the originator." That is related to the fact that even though we "measure" our ingredients today, we still don't follow the rules of exact measurement.

Unless you weigh your ingredients, measuring is somewhat the same. Let's say you measure a cup of flour. Then you sift and resift and sift again. Then re-measure to see what it actually is. That may be different than someone who measures their flour straight from the bin and never sifts or slightly sifts. Each ingredient is measured differently from person to person, hence the inconsistency between results.

Fannie Farmer in her original book tells how to measure thus: "Correct measurements are absolutely necessary." She doesn't say that you can fudge it and use your own methods; she says, "absolutely necessary," with her going on to say, "to ensure the best results." If you are making a recipe for the first time, it is best to follow it to a "T," as described in Fannie's and in Meta's cookbooks. Fannie gives a suggestion to purchase your "kitchen furnishing," which we call utensils, at a specific store that sells the items, not to use just any "furnishing" you like.

Fannie's information specifies "tin measuring-cups, divided in quarters or thirds ... and tea and table spoons of regulation sizes." These are not the sizes we use at the table that come with our silverware set. If you use the silverware tablespoon and measure that compared to a regulation tablespoon, you will find that it is a bit different. That is why when asking for a teaspoon, don't use your silverware, as the size is not a "regulation size."

With each ingredient, Fannie gives specific instructions where dry ingredients "should be sifted before measuring." If you are taking an ingredient from a box like mustard, Fannie says it "should be stirred to lighten" as items are known to settle to the bottom. "A cupful is measured level," which means use a measuring cup specifically made to level off the top with a kitchen or "case knife."

However, with all of these wonderful instructions by Fannie, Meta and others, there were still individuals who followed the recipe that measured the flour in the "cup" of their hand or a pinch using their fingers as their measuring utensil. They either still used the recipe and method out of frugality or habit that was passed down from one generation to another. Some recipes are just too endearing to give up, knowing that your "great" grandmother used that specific recipe.

Between 1796 to 1876, close to 100 years of publishing cookbooks, over 1,000 were printed officially in the United States. They were full-blown cookbooks or simple little pamphlets, but they helped change the way Americans cooked for their families. They learned about medicinal remedies as well as food recipes.

Fannie Farmer wrote her first cookbook in 1896 some 20 years later. She said, "Progress in civilization has been accompanied by progress in cookery." She was right on so many levels. Every time there was a step forward in the way we processed food, whether it was fields of grains or the cooking of foods, the progress of the population improved dramatically. Once we had the written word, you could see the progress go hand in hand.

# MY TIME WITH META GIVEN

Fannie Farmer started teaching at Harvard's Boston Cooking School. She was the first female teacher in the early 1900s. It was an all-male class. Female students went to Vassar starting in 1861. This invitation was to teach cooking to doctors and nurses. She had also started her own cooking school. She wrote two important cookbooks, amongst others. The first book included nutrition and diet, but most importantly, it contained the accurate measurement of ingredients. The second book concentrated on proper food for the sick. She had the most knowledge regarding the proper presentation of food for the ill to help their appetites.

Fannie had other cookbooks, but those two were her most noted. For her, she had a special affinity for her second cookbook called *Food and Cookery for the Sick and Convalescent* in 1904. She had suffered as a child and was unable to initially continue her education. When she gained her health, she was able to continue and studied at the Boston Cooking School. She worked right up until her death at the age of 57 in 1915.

The ending of Fannie's life marked the beginning of Meta Given's home economic career direction by finishing up her first year at the University of Chicago. As one life was ending, another picked up the reins and carried the torch, in the ever-burning need for scientific cookery.

Another famous but small cookbook was called *Rumford Cookbook,* which was written by Lily Haworth Wallace. She emigrated to the United

States from England in 1900. She was a specialist in home economics, lecturing and teaching cooking skills to women throughout the country. She wrote a dozen other cookbooks. The little *Rumford Complete Cookbook* had some forty-two publishings over a span of forty years, with five million copies. This important but little book had a various number of pages from as many as 260 to as few as 213 pages over the years. If you could only have one cookbook and did not want to spend much, then this would be the book for you.

Many times, these books were something you sent away for or came with Rumford Baking Powder. It was updated over the years. It was very popular and there has been a republishing of the book in 2010 by Kessinger Publishing, LLC (September 10, 2010).

Then there was the little cookbook by Irma Rombauer, the empress of the *Joy of Cooking* cookbook, which she self-published in 1931 after losing her husband and all hope of an income. This was a very important cookbook and is still managed by her great-grandchildren.

Through these and many other cookbooks that have been kept alive, we have been able to cook the best food possible for our families. We entertain at established and new venues through their help and guidance, with some of our fondest memories from television shows like Julia Childs.

Meta Given like so many other cookbook authors, left their mark on the American fabric with their mighty cookbooks. The preserving of these books has become the project of many a college and university. The telling and retelling of their importance and significance has opened our eyes to review the past and bring that information into the forefront for all to understand. One cannot really understand their present and go forth into the future without knowing the past.

Lest we forget or ignore the important work of the women who came before, the work of millions of women and their never-ending efforts over the centuries has so often been glossed over and treated like it was not important.

When we look at history, you can name hundreds of men who came before, but we only have a fraction of those numbers of women remembered for their names and deeds, as if there were so few of us who made any contributions. Try these names out for size:

Amelia Simmons, Fannie Merritt Farmer, Irma Rombauer, Catherine Beecher and Harriet Beecher Stowe, Ellen Swallow Richards, "Aunt Babette", Minerva C. Fox, Marion Harland, Estelle Woods Wilcox, Sara Bosse, Watanna Onoto, Janet McKenzie, Miss Parloa, Eleanor Parkinson, Mrs. N. K. M. Lee, Celestine Eustis, Eliza Leslie, Martha McCulloch Williams, Elizabeth E. Lea, Bertha M. Wood, Lydia Maria Francis Child, Susannah Carter, Sarah Josepha Buell Hale, Isabel Gordon Curtis, Anna Maria Collins, Henriette Davidis, Ann Allen, Marion Fontaine Cabell Tyree, Florence Kreisler Greenbaum, Maria Gentile, Jane Cunningham Croly, Sarah Josepha Buell Hale, Eliza Leslie, Edith M.

Thomas, Jane Eayre Fryer, Juliet Corson, Miss Parloa, Mary Johnson Lincoln, Sarah Tyson Rorer, Maria Eliza Rundell, Lucy Montpelier Emerson, Esther Allen Howland, Mary F. Henderson, Elizabeth Fries Ellet, Mary W. Hinman Abel, Eliza Leslie, Mary Randolph, Linda Deziah Jennings, Abby Fisher, Adelaide Keen, Fanny Lemira Gillette, Adelaide Keen, and Mrs. Hattie A. Burr.

Fifty-six women wrote most of the seventy-five books that are collected on the Michigan "Feeding America" website. Many of these women we have not heard of and their names have been lost in the history of our nation. Yet the Michigan "Feeding America" project deemed these books written by these women as the most important for a variety of reasons.

We know now that Amelia Simmons wrote the first American cookbook. We have identified that Fannie Merritt Farmer wrote two of the most important cookbooks, one with exact measurements and the other regarding the feeding of the ill and the importance of presentation.

Catharine Esther Beecher and her sister Harriet wrote a very important scientific book dedicated to the American woman. They were interested in the latest of inventions, the new setups based on these inventions and they were fore thinkers when it came to understand that the servant might go the way of the dodo bird.

"Aunt Babette" wrote a non-kosher Jewish cookbook that held the test of time for over 25 years starting in 1889. Minnie C. Fox wrote an "authentic"

Kentucky cookbook that instructed how to make pickled tomatoes, punch with bourbon whisky, and many things with corn, including dodgers, cake and pudding.

Estelle Woods Wilcox took a cookbook with her from Ohio to Minneapolis, enhanced the book and published it with her introductions. She was able to help a charity in Ohio realize their dream to raise $2,000 for their parsonage.

Marion Harland (Mary Virginia Terhune) wrote two cookbooks that included her personalized chatter at the beginning of chapters and sometimes throughout the recipe. It sounds like some of Meta Given's type of chatter that she provided at the beginning of her chapters. Marion was a famous author with "Alone" being one of her best loved books in the 1800s.

Janet McKenzie Hill and Miss Parloa wrote a book about chocolate. These women were celebrities in their day as culinary cooks and authors as well as editors – it is noted that this was uncommon, but as we are finding, this is more common than is believed as you can see by the fifty-six names mentioned above.

Marion Harland wrote *Common Sense In The Household: A Manual Of Practical Housewifery*. This book is deemed important for its Southern cuisine with national appeal in the 1870s. She is the author of two cookbooks that were widely popular in the day. She tried to convey to the reader that she "understood exactly what they were going through" and that if they took her advice she could help guide them through their daily drudgeries. Again, it sounds a lot like our Meta, who believed that her cookbooks were a second pair of hands in every task of your household chores.

*The Complete Confectioner, Pastry-Cook And Baker* was written by Eleanor Parkinson. She was one of the foremost confectioners in the Philadelphia area. Much of this book was borrowed from an English cookbook, yet another celebrity cook in her day. Mrs. N. K. M. Lee wrote the first alphabetized cookbook, which she heavily borrowed from British cookeries. Her book called *The Cook's Own Book: Being A Complete Culinary Encyclopedia* also had the word encyclopedia within its title, much like Meta Given's Encyclopedia of Cooking, which also was alphabetized.

Celestine Eustis wrote *Cooking in Old Creole Days* with many wonderful recipes from New Orleans and much credit given to African Americans. There is a statement which reads "the Strength of the nation lies in the hands of the cook." Many pleasing illustrations throughout the book are by Harper Pennington. This is a bilingual book in English and French.

Eliza Leslie is yet another cookbook author celebrity who wrote many cookbooks, including *Directions For Cookery which went through some sixty publishings in about thirty years. She was very popular because she believed in honesty and integrity of ingredients. She spoke of cooking nuances in an eloquent and down to earth writing style. She talked about the importance of using good measurements down to half a jill (gill), which is referred to as ½ cup or ¼ of a pint.*

# MY TIME WITH META GIVEN

*With little ditties like this, I believe it is a true American classic.*

*Each book has a brief introduction to tell us a little about the author, the times they lived in, and something that makes their book worthy of the University of Michigan's Feeding America project.*

*I have not been able to do this project justice as there are seventy-five books, and I find I do not have the time nor the inclination to read these lovely books thoroughly. However, I hope I have given you enough of a flavor to entice you to peruse their digital stack for old-time recipes and remedies for fun or for the making of a new family favorite.*

Much of the problem with our history is we lose the benefit of really important historical figures who helped shape our nation in little known ways. We just dismiss their efforts completely, like they didn't exist. Meta Hortense Given was a major contributor from 1925 until 1972 with forty-seven years of research, testing, writing, and down-to-earth demonstrations. Her work was washed away like it meant nothing – yet she single-handedly fed a nation during two World Wars through frugality with maximum nutritional value as a *home economist*.

All told, Meta Given had a seventy-year career where she taught school-age children at various stages in their lives through college. That was twenty-two years she simultaneously went to school and worked.

Then she spent from 1925 until 1972 scientifically analyzing food for its content. She wrote as a journalist, as a cookbook author, as a syndicated columnist or performing demonstrations. Her cookbooks are her living legacy. May we all be so lucky to leave such a lasting and enduring product.

When we talk about cookbook history, please don't leave out one of the most prolific writers of our time from 1925 to 1972. Meta Given will rise again if I have anything to say about it. And if I have to do all the work to bring her back from the brink of extinction, I will. It's hard to believe that someone of such great import can be forgotten. But it seems that this has happened to so many wonderful women over the centuries.

Thanks to news organizations like Huffington Post and others, the web has brought so many women back into our history. We need to learn about these women and so many other remarkable individuals who have been eradicated from our history. History is made all the richer by putting these people back into the story we tell about our past, just because.

This chapter is my hope to liberate all of the cookbooks that came before Meta Given's cookbook. This is to thank everyone who labored over each cookbook, labored over each recipe, labored over all the testing and tasting. I am grateful to all of them for taking the time to share their life's work that became the culmination of all that Meta Given learned through her studies. Without many of them, we might not have had such a wonderful legacy left by our ingenious Meta Given.

It has been a privilege and an honor to spend these past few years researching the old data of Meta Given's life. To go back and bring her to life and put her in her rightful place in history: as one of the most forward-thinking *scientific home economists* of her time.

She did not give up until she had learned all she could learn, until she provided every last soldier with the food that made them strong and help bring them back from war to build this nation into what it was through the '50s and '60s. While they built America, she fed them nutritious, delicious, economical meals.

She came into my life through my mother who learned her craft at the elbow of Meta Given in her humble kitchen in the early 1950s. While Meta did not stand directly next to my mother, Meta did provide her with a second pair of hands with every word that my mother absorbed while reading through the good basic knowledge that Meta provided.

My mother and her sister used the famed *Meta Given's Encyclopedia of Cooking* cookbook and both became very accomplished chefs in their own right. There seems to be nothing they could not cook: meat of every kind and description, cookies, pies, cakes and homemade white bread. Those cooking lessons were passed down to the next generation.

My brother Will, sister Sue, myself and Reg and Kelly continue a family tradition of baking. Will makes the best bread and rolls ever eaten. My sister Sue carried on the traditions and the many lessons learned at our mother's elbow, which were the lessons our mother learned from Meta Given. Sue has gone on the make some of the best gluten-free products this world has ever experienced.

Our beloved Jamie went to culinary school, and with the lessons he learned at his auntie's elbow (my mother) after school, he went on to be a beautiful Chef and Hotel Manager. As for me, I learned to cook at my mother's elbow and learned to cook mostly without the recipe book with the exception of baked goods.

Now we have the next generation in the young lady to whom this chapter is dedicated to. She is carrying the torch for all of us. She has left our kitchen, cooking the humble dishes of our family to culinary school. She went on to study at Lincoln Culinary in Hartford Connecticut. She has worked at several restaurants in the state of Connecticut.

In the telling of Meta Given's story through their meals, each person has kept her alive with their continuous use of her cookbooks that have held up to the test of time. Meta left no stone unturned in her cookbooks. While they did not contain everything, Meta tried to cover all of the subjects that helped with the basics and with thorough knowledge of many of the very important subjects necessary for the student, the new cook and even the seasoned chef. Her books were so comprehensive that she even talked about the kitchen sink. Some subjects we are hard pressed to find in another cookbook written today or even yesteryear.

There are many wonderful cooks, chefs and authors who have not been mentioned in this chapter, but this chapter is only to give you a flavor of the long history of cookbooks. It took over 100 years to publish 1,000 books in America's history, since Amelia first rolled her cookbook off the printing press some 200 years ago. Today, in one year, there are thousands of cookbooks published every year.

Walk into a bookstore and you will find the shelves stocked with hundreds of cookbooks. Within the bookshelves of a used bookstore there are plenty of bookshelves just dedicated to cookbooks. These represent only a fraction of all the cookbooks that sit upon our shelves. Whether amateur or professional.

And let us not forget about the Internet, dedicated to recipes, digital cookbooks and all the blogs that relay stories about their favorite chefs, cookbook authors and their own tales about cooking.

The writing of a cookbook is a tremendous undertaking. Never underestimate the amount of work that goes into writing such grand books as were written back at the turn of the twentieth century. This writing of cookbooks was dominated by women. Women also dominated writing for newspapers, teaching and secretarial work. They could have dominated scientific work as well, but they were shut out from those fields or kept at "computer" levels.

Those are human computers, as they were called back in the day. It meant they did much of the cataloging in the field, such as of the stars in the sky. Annie Jump Cannon (December 11, 1863 – April 13, 1941) was an accomplished scientist. She was an

American astronomer whose cataloging work was instrumental in the development of contemporary stellar classification.

*The Ladies Home Journal* was started in 1883 and the *Good House Keeping* magazine started in 1885. Both of these began before Meta Given was born. She became part of their history and they become part of her legacy. Meta Given was never given credit for the pictures that show up in these magazines and journals through her tenure from the early 1930s to the late 1940s. She nonetheless was there with her articles, her photographs and her consultations for these famous venues as well as many others, as documented in her own interviews over the years.

Cookbooks changed the way we did our cooking. They helped feed us when we were hungry. They were enlightening, and they were our saviors. But most of all, they were there at every turn in our history for thousands of years.

Regardless of the audience, they were there. For years, women were prevented from learning to read, so we passed our precious recipes down through word of mouth, through the touch and feel of the product in our hands.

We were never truly stopped from learning the craft, because we were the ones who fed our nations and kept each other strong. Women are the ones who provided most of the food. Even though men went out hunting, it was women who found ways to prepare food even in the leanest of times.

We are the innovators. We are the inventors. We are true providers of life. When you educate a man, you educate an individual. When you educate a woman, you feed (educate) the world -- Dr. James Emmanuel Kwegyir-Aggrey (1875-1927).

Let the cookbook be your guide – get out there and cook something, for the love of family!

# Chapter Six

## From the Encyclopedia

*Dedicated to my dear sweet Auntie, Ethel Anna*

META Given wrote so many wonderful passages in her books. She starts chapters out with great descriptions about the subject at hand, including a bit of pop culture: "If I'd known you were coming, I'd have baked you a cake," or a bit of history: "Food is more readily available than your mother or grandmother ever thought of... "

I am sharing some of her writings from her cookbook. I have chosen the 1952 and 1953 cookbook called *Meta Given's Encyclopedia of Cooking*. She wrote two versions with several copyrights - 1947, 1948, 1949, 1952, 1953; in the 1955 there are two volumes in one book, but only 1947, 1955, 1959, 1966, 1969 in the 1969 two volumes. There is a discrepancy in the copyrighted versions of her book. However, the one I am going to be referencing is the 1952 single volume book that has the copyright documented.

In Meta Given's acknowledgment, which starts out acknowledging the effort involved in creating this cookbook, it says it took over two years to formulate the information Meta Given had compiled. The book and the people involved was a full effort which included materials, cooking, tasting and so many other labors. *"Building a cook book is much like building a house in that both must be large, functional and modern enough to serve one's needs for practical and pleasant ways of living."*

This part reminds me of when my daughter asked me how a house was built. We used to go by this house every day when she was about four years old. Each day I would tell her in more detail how a house was built. I see Meta knew a thing or two about how to build a house. Her equation of building a house and a cookbook are uncanny. *"First the builder goes through a stage of dreaming ..."*

I love the simplicity of an actually very complicated process. When Meta Given decided to write a cookbook, she already had much of the material gathered. I remember reading that she had collected cookbooks, articles and her own notes over the years. I read about one of the first cookbooks she used, which came to them through a periodical called *Journal of Agriculture*. This periodical provided cookbooks, the first mentioned by Meta Given in a 1941 article in the *St. Louis Dispatch*. *"When he finally decides to build his house, a blue print is drawn ..."*

Interesting how Meta talks about the decision to make the house, then realizes that you need to create a blueprint. Does that mean that Meta Given put together an outline of what she wanted her cookbook to be when completed? I gather Meta was organized, she was thorough, and she was always glad to collaborate with other experts in the field.

Meta Given mentioned twenty-five people who helped her accomplish her finished cookbook. That's a lot of collaboration, testing and tweaking of something not so simple as a 1,700-page cookbook.

Which she continues to revise for twenty-five years from about 1947 through 1972.

So many times, Meta Given reminds us that the work we do in the home is no different than work that is done outside the home. That the importance of work is no less important than anyone else's work: the builder of a home, the architect, the contractor, or the mason.

She believed that the work provided at home could easily be equated with work in any other job. In the above example, she was talking about her own work in creating her cookbook. But we know from her articles that she felt the same way with housework, cooking and the many other tasks that women performed to manage a household we all call home.

This first chapter from the book I am going to reference was renamed a few times before it became the condensed name of *The Diet Pattern*. The chapter provides basic information about the diet pattern that was information not readily available but was required by the Food and Nutrition Board of the National Research Council.

Meta tried through many of her writings, demonstrations and books to convey this information to the masses. Also, her cookbooks were used at universities across the nation. So, this information was necessary for a home economics education from the *Encyclopedia,* as many people reference her encyclopedic cookbook today.

The diet pattern will provide us with all *"the facts about food and its nutritive value."* that is presented to use in Meta's own "down-to-earth manner," with narratives of the intricacies as Meta takes you into her laboratory in such a way that reveals your very own humble kitchen's ability to provide the family with exuberant well-being through a "well-chosen diet!"

As time goes by, the information keeps its value. Why do we throw away the old and replace with the new? Only history can tell us the value of that tradition. I know that many people believe in the successful study of the past in detail. Therefore, this cookbook's information is of excellent value and should be taught repeatedly through the rest of time. Like listening to an old song enjoyed by each generation, this helps us understand the past, comprehend what needs to be done today, and guides us into our future endeavors.

"The 365 daily menus used in this book have been built to include the basic foods which supply the normal individual's daily needs..." "All of your needs" includes protein, or the very important minerals and the expensive vitamins that Meta believes are like gold.

And don't forget the level of energy that proper food provides. The menus Meta prepared were the latest according to "the diet pattern of the day." This included ten classifications of various foods that should be eaten throughout the day.

The 365 daily menus have three meals provided in detail. Wow! We just don't do that kind of thing today. We repetitively eat the same thing over and over. As a matter of fact, some people eat the same thing every Saturday for dinner as they have for the past 30 years or so. Can you imagine eating something different for just about every meal for a period of 365 days? I know I could not. But how wonderful it would be to accomplish that! And think of all the great nutrition you would be receiving.

Those 10 food classifications from Meta's reference manual in the cookbook included milk for all family members, regardless of how they were prepared or consumed; meat included poultry and fish and don't forget about liver.

There are vegetables which she has two classifications green and yellow and non-green and yellow. Fruit was also broken into two groups citrus and tomato and non-citrus inclusive of all varieties. Potatoes were thought to be very important, and pasta and rice were poor substitutions.

Do not forget about eggs several times a week. Butter or fortified margarine got its own group. And of course, whole grains, and note the word whole. Meta tells us that is was after the Civil War that we fell in love with white bread and white sugar. (Unknown, 1941)

Meta Given believed that there were basic groups that you should include in each meal, yet you could mix and match those foods to come up with literally 365 different meal combinations. Which really equates to 1,095 different meals in the year.

Amazing! I know for me, cooking all those different meals would be a lot of extra work. I usually try to make a casserole, soup or some other combination that will provide meals for several days running. Leftovers are great, and I can't imagine somehow juggling my schedule to include cooking three meals a day.

It is not always easy to include the ten basics in our diet today. They are broken up about the same today as they were then. However, something like milk is not required to be consumed with each meal daily. While children still do drink milk if they can tolerate it, I am not sure it is always fit in. I know that we did not insist our daughter drink milk with each meal. However, it was something that we gave to her in-between meals and at bedtime.

Now I see why we don't eat pasta or rice very often. It was not recommended to be eaten on a regular basis because it did not provide as much nutrition as other things like potatoes. Even though I have read articles of late that say potatoes make you gain weight. I have also read other articles that say potatoes aid in weight loss or maintenance. As with everything – if eaten in moderation, about all foods are a benefit. *"The basic foods should be selected not for food value alone, but also for texture, color and flavor contrast."*

Meta Given was very concerned with food's appeal and texture as well as its nutritional value. If you did not like a food, or it was not appealing, what is the point of eating it? Many people are fussy about their food. But Meta believed that if you cooked a food properly and presented it in an appealing fashion, you might be more likely to eat just about anything.

Meta Given was a great advocate of substitutions. This works perfectly today. There are so many reasons to make a substitution – celiac disease, food allergies, seasonal availability or even pricing concerns. I have found that some of the best gluten-free foods are Meta's recipes with substitutions. For instance, I have made her biscuit recipe substituting out the flour or the milk as our family needs gluten-free foods and I need milk-free foods. Never underestimate the power of the older recipes that still hold up to the test of time regardless of the changes you must make to keep up with your own needs.

*"A well-balanced diet is made up of a great variety of foods, from which the body obtains the elements it requires for growth, maintenance and repair."*

Meta talks about *"hidden hunger."* This is not when you don't eat or you don't get enough to eat, necessarily. It's when what you eat does not have the proper nutrition or the nutrition is not absorbed into your body properly. Celiac disease and food allergies(sensitivities) can cause this issue, but so can eating foods that just don't provide nutrition. Meta wrote at great length about how different food elements could help with the building of the body from protein, carbohydrates, fats, minerals, vitamins, and of course bulk, which is all aided with water.

Here is an amazing science lesson on the acidity and alkaline properties of food. This is a problem for people who don't understand. We often think that acidic food is just that when we eat it. But our bodies convert it to be alkaline. Now there's a conundrum. We need the acid to convert to alkaline. So, if you worry about not having the proper pH balance of foods, eat your fruits and vegetables (eight or nine daily), and you will probably get the proper balance.

I found an interesting article on the Internet that outlined eight ridiculous myths about meat and health. The good, the bad and the not so ugly, as it turns out. Meta Given was a great advocate of meat. So, eat up. (Gunnars, 2014)

Acid and Alkaline Foods
"Foods rich in protein, such as meat, eggs and fish exert an acid effect in the body. When protein burns in the body, the end-products are uric acid, sulfuric acid and phosphoric acid. These acids become harmless because they are neutralized or balanced with alkaline salts in the body to form neutral salts, which are excreted by the kidneys."

I found this interesting blog called "The Alkaline or Acid Effect of Food," which is very close to the original material Meta Given has provided in this informative information within her cookbook. Curiously, this appears to have been copied from her book with a few words from the author.

*"Most fruits and vegetables tend to produce an alkaline effect in the body because they contain calcium, sodium, potassium and magnesium salts, all of which are alkaline. As stated above, these salts neutralize the acids that are the end-products resulting from the chemical changes that proteins undergo in the body."*

You don't have to be overwhelmed by the fact that you can't retain this information for future proper nutrition. Just stick to the basics, with about a quarter of your plate of meat, a half of vegetables or fruit and the last portion has potatoes, rice or pasta if you feel the need.

*"The acids in apples (malic), in sauerkraut (lactic), in grapes (tartaric), and in lemons and oranges (citric), oxidize in the body to become carbonic acid, which is expelled from the body in the breath."*

We may not always understand the type of acids in foods, but on a daily basis, it is not necessary. Isn't it great that Meta provides us with this detail? She believed in mixing up the way you got all the different types of acids, proteins, carbs, fats and the like. Meta took the guessing out of *what's for dinner*? With her menus, you were covered. Even if you substituted and stuck to the recommended substitutions again, you were covered.

I was also interested to know a little bit more about quinic acid as she wrote about this acid, which I had not heard of before. The Wikipedia page gives us additional information. What I find fascinating is that it is found in the lovely foods that are natural. They talk about how they are using this acid to find cures for various illness. But one of the issues with natural is that method is out. We need to fabricate everything.

*"Other organic acids such as benzoic and quinic present in fruits such as cranberries, plums and prunes are not oxidized in the usual way; their final effect is acid, even though neutral salts are present. Therefore, the taste of a food or the original acidity does not indicate its final effect in the body."*

# MY TIME WITH META GIVEN

This cookbook's wealth of information makes it my first go-to resource for cooking, healthy eating and all things about food. Just this section on acid and alkaline is chock-a-block full of details you would be hard-pressed to find in any one resource.

"Oxalic acid, which is found in rhubarb, chard, beet greens, spinach (but not in mustard or turnip greens) in cocoa and tea is poorly oxidized." I have never heard of anyone else talking about oxalic acid. Today it is a lost art to really break down food.

*"The presence of oxalic acid in the body prevents the utilization of an equivalent amount of calcium."* I have often heard that spinach has calcium, but according to this information. You need to digest it with other foods that have the proper use of calcium. *"Therefore, when such foods as rhubarb and spinach are eaten, a liberal supply of calcium should be provided by foods such as milk, cheese, beans and cabbage."*

As you read more thoroughly about each one of these acids, elements, proteins, etc., you find that we should have all of these to help the body remain in balance. It is never any one element or item that is needed; it is all to protect that delicate dance we play with nature. No one seemed to know more about this than Meta Given, the scientist.

*"The bicarbonates, phosphates and proteins which are always present in the blood serve as balancing agents or buffers and protect the tissues and blood against sudden changes in their normal, faintly alkaline reaction."* Wow, I feel like I am getting a scientific education, just reading this cookbook.

*"These alkaline reserves may become depleted, but the body actually does not become acid in reaction."* So never

underestimate your food that is farm fresh minus GMO, hormones and the like. Don't be afraid to get back to the basics and notice the difference in your food bill and medical bill when you get as close to natural as possible.

If Meta Given were with us today, she would be admonishing the new status quo. She worked very hard to help people figure out why we are getting diabetes, heart disease, and why so many are dying. She would be on top of why so many of us have allergies to the very food that is supposed to be saving our lives instead of taking it. *"A normal, healthy body is equipped to utilize efficiently the foods eaten, regardless of acid or alkaline properties."*

After all, per Meta Given's advice, with this delicate dance our bodies have with proper diets, we should not be having the issues we encounter today. So many healthy people are dying from the very foods that were so perfectly made to make us healthy and normal.

Meta used all kinds of sources to obtain her information. She had access to more resources because she also provided much needed details through her consulting business, "Meta Given's Scientific Kitchens" out of Chicago from 1933-1948.

Meta Given on freezing foods: *"Even though frozen foods do retain the fine qualities of the fresh products to a high degree, it must also be remembered that freezing does not improve an underripe berry, or a mealy, bland flavored peach."* The best quality of food should be used no matter the processing such as canning,

# MY TIME WITH META GIVEN

frozen, or fresh. *"The quality of the frozen foods can never be any better than that of the original food."*

Meta Given tried in her humble example to demonstrate why you should use freezing methods, but don't under or overestimate the power of freezing our foods. However, while it will never be better than the quality of the original food, freezing is a great way to preserve food to as close as possible to the original for a much longer period of time than just trying to store the food in the refrigerator or cold storage.

*"In any type of food preservation, a considerable amount of money, labor, and time is invested, and it is poor economy to use anything but the best available product that is most suited for the process."* Great advice no matter the project at hand. It is not always easy to see the result, but if you take the time and effort, then the result will be well worth the proper planning. I cannot tell you enough that reading the instructions are worth the time and effort.

Many people cannot understand why they failed until they reread the instructions and realize knowing the ending is just as important at the beginning. *"Since high quality for the different kinds of fruits, meats, and vegetables cannot be described in general terms..."* Meta provides many tables which give you the details that assist with the full understanding of what is meant by different kinds of quality.

Meta Given does provide several tables of information about the specific foods for freezing. She goes to great efforts to prove the exact information about what and how. Certain foods are not suitable at all for freezing. The advice is best adhered to otherwise all your efforts and your hard-earned money will have been for naught.

Canning, Preserving and Pickling

You have to love reading how Meta Given phrases her opening paragraph in such a way that you can see and feel exactly as Meta felt about this particular experience – that first delighted moment, then the applause, and the gratification.

*"It's a proud moment when you open the first jar of your very own peaches, pickles, strawberry jam, or luscious red tomato juice!"* Having been the benefactor of this moment as a child, eating my mother's efforts or doing this myself, I know well the moment that Meta is talking about.

*"Even if you've never canned before, it will be easy when you've read this chapter."* The last part of this sentence says it all: "it will be easy." While I must say it is not easy by any stretch of the imagination, the reward and repetition of the effort will make it easy over time.

I have canned many a food, and I do agree that today I find it easier than the first time I performed the task. It is true that learning with Meta standing next to me through her instructions in her cookbooks, she makes it so very much easier. Her instructions are step by step, and she never lets you down with a missed detail.

Meta Given's information gives you the why you can - because it is economical. She gives you the visible reasoning - colorful rows. And she gives you the purpose to have pride in the finished results. Who wouldn't want to follow her advice and come up with the best results so that you can brag about what you have done, show it off for company and your family?

*"Canning is one of the most economical ways to preserve foods, and colorful rows of home-canned fruits and vegetables give visible evidence of a homemaker's skill, thrift, and nutrition-wise planning."* Meta's advice in all things relating to food, homemaking and the kitchen is advice you can rely on no matter the task, and advice that you can use into the workforce.

I have often believed that if you have a successful home business, you can make it in the business world outside the home. Because anyone who has run a successful home and worked in business knows that the latter is much easier than the home business.

*"Actually, the qualifications for successful canning are the same as those required in every phase of homemaking - cleanliness, intelligent management, the ability to follow directions accurately, and the will to see a job carried through to a successful finish."*

Canning became available to us at the turn of the eighteenth century. The basic principles have remained the same for well over a century. While not as many people can as they did in the past. One of the latest crazes is using "mason" jars for everything.

You can use them to freeze, or just a tight container to transport your food from point A to point B. They also now come with handles and all kinds of covers. Even a cover with lights that can be used out of doors for a decorative light powered by the sun.

Homemaker's Handbook for Buying Staples

This section of Meta Given's cookbook is chock full of facts about your everyday staples that we don't think much about, but there is a lot of information that can make the difference of ordinary to extraordinary in your purchasing and finished product.

Not only will this information be helpful in your cooking, but also in your dining-out experience. You may be able to tell the difference between various items just from having read this chapter and the explanation that is given by your waitstaff for certain items on the menu.

*"This chapter is a series of handy reference guides designed to answer your questions about various staple items. We have included in these foods, chocolate and cocoa, fats, oils, and other shortenings, flours, leavening agents, milk and milk products, nuts, olives and pickles, sugars and syrups, and spices, herbs, extracts, and vinegars."*

If you are going to use Meta Given's books, treat them like a novel or a thorough instruction manual and read the specified section carefully before attempting new avenues in cooking. Once I realized that her books were instruction manuals, this helped enlighten me to their full potential.

Then I realized that the information she was imparting was to make you an expert in the area of cooking that you wished to accomplish. My family

# MY TIME WITH META GIVEN

have been using these instructions for well over sixty years, with the greatest of success.

*"It is more factual material than you would probably enjoy reading at one stretch, but every page contains facts about commonly used foods, that would be of interest and practical help to everyone who is buying food, or planning to buy it one day."*

Today we often don't bother with the details that are provided in this chapter or many of the chapters within Meta Given's cookbooks. However, I know that we do seek the answers, but we look them up piecemeal from the Internet, never realizing the importance of having all this information in one guide.

*"Just a casual turning of the next ten or fifteen pages will bring to your attention numerous little-known facts about many of these foods, and we feel sure, will encourage you to turn to these pages often when you are seeking an answer to some question."*

Needless to say, I now use this book as my first reference when looking for guidance on all subjects of food. I looked through many books about chocolate and when I finally read this chapter, all of my chocolate answers were revealed. I should have started here instead of ending here.

The above paragraph and this one below gives us great advice both about the fact that her cookbook is full of information and that you need to take your time to absorb all the details provided. I know my mother read a section as was needed at the time.

For instance, she read the details about making bread and later helped one of the neighbor girls with that very chapter to make her first loaf of bread.

Below, the information is about spices. Meta provide detail, charts and suggestions of how to use, when to use and sometimes when not to use.

"*Remember these pages when you are tasting an exotic dish in an unusual restaurant: the spice chart will suggest the spice to go with different kinds of foods.*" This spice chart that she offers will give you great depth regarding many different spices. It may not encompass all spices, but it is a great starting point.

"*Remember these pages when you are wondering how cocoa is made, or why you can keep the hydrogenated shortenings at room temperature, or the difference between brown sugar, granulated, powdered, and confectioners'.*"

I have had many a question about the next subject. Who doesn't want to know more about chocolate? It's certainly one of my favorite ingredients for cookies, cakes and other sweets.

Answers to Questions About Chocolate…Cocoa

"*Chocolate and Cocoa are produced from the roasted beans of cacao trees, grown in the tropical belt near the equator … Chocolate is made by grinding the fermented, roasted, shelled cacao beans …*"

This information is so timeless. I have read much about chocolate in trying to make my own chocolates. As usual, I should have come to the *Encyclopedia* written by Meta Given in 1947 first. It is one of the best resources for so many basic but complicated food subjects. Finally, she explained in detail the variances in the types of chocolates.

"*The difference between Bitter, Semi-sweet, Sweet, and Milk Chocolate is based on the amount of sugar and milk that is added to the chocolate. Bitter chocolate 5 to 20 percent sugar, Semi-sweet 20 to 40 percent sugar, and Sweet 40 to 65 percent sugar. Milk chocolate contains 12 percent whole milk solids and 35 to 50 percent sugar. Cocoa is made by removing about one-half of the cocoa butter from the ground chocolate. The remaining mixture contains about 22 percent of the original cocoa butter. It is allowed to harden into a cake and is then pulverized into cocoa powder."*

One of the things I have always wanted to know is what is Dutch chocolate? Now the mystery of this term has been explained so simply, you'd think I should have known that before. Yum on the Dutch chocolate beverages; now I know why some are smoother than others.

*"Dutch process cocoa is chemically treated to darken and enrich the color. Dutch process cocoa is also said to dissolve more easily and has less tendency to settle out when made into a beverage."*

The following paragraph really helps with understanding the differences of cocoa and chocolate. People have always used these interchangeably, but they cannot be interchanged without making a difference in the process of cocoa as opposed to baking chocolate. Now I feel so much better informed than before, just with this one little paragraph. Knowledge is power in getting it right when trying to figure out if you can use one ingredient or another as a substitute.

*"Cocoa and chocolate may be used interchangeably ... Three level tablespoons of cocoa plus two teaspoons of shortening are ... one ounce of baking chocolate. Chocolate ... melt over hot water, microwave or cut and*

*added to liquid and heated until it melts, cooled and added to the other ingredients. Cocoa ... sifted with dry ingredients or mixed with cold liquid and stirred until smooth and then added to the remaining ingredients."*

As with all of Meta's instructions, she makes sure you understand how to store this all-important and expensive ingredient. You can't just leave it lying on the counter or in a house that is not properly tempered. If you don't use AC in the summertime, you can adversely affect many foods. So, heed Meta's advice regarding the proper storage of all foods.

Chocolate starts degrading when kept at the wrong temperature above a certain temperature, like 85 degrees or more. You know when it turns that funky gray color and sometime crumbles? That's when the ingredients separate. Meta suggests trying to keep your chocolate in a well-tempered house.

I wished I had read this information when I was learning to make chocolates. I did look for recipes, but I somehow missed the information section. Meta tried to cover all bases when it came to food. I just learned by looking at the wiki webpage that it's been around for several millennia and is enjoyed by many cultures coming from Mexico and other regions in that area (Chocolate, 2017).

There is so much confusion about the next subject – fats. We have been told to avoid them at all costs. But as time goes by, we are learning that different fats are good for us. I believe in the old adage, "all things in moderation." Meta was of the same belief. She gives you as up-to-date information as she had at the time. Today we also have information about partially hydrogenated fats.

Her book section is titled *The answers to your questions about fats, oils and other shortenings*. I believe Meta would have various other things to say about fats and oils today. We have had a love affair with them, we have put them on the bad list, and now we are reassessing the true value and needs of these different fats.

I don't believe we can live without fat nor should we, but on the other hand, we need to be mindful of all the foods we eat, and the portion of the food they have within the finished product.

The art of the information in the chapter *Homemaker Handbook for Purchasing Fruits and Vegetables* is all but lost. I never notice different grades of fruits and vegetables. As far as seasons go, there seems to be no seasons when it comes to fruits and vegetables today.

After all you can pretty much get all fruits and vegetables all year round. However, have you noticed that some are on sale at different times of the year? For instance, strawberries are cheapest around the end of June to the beginning of July. That is because they are actually in season at that time of year.

One should heed the words of Meta Given as she researched and scientifically prepared this and all her chapters with years of study. One of the great things about her cookbook is, she continued to research and kept updating her books over the years. Within her advice she asks us to notice that food is not always what you expect.

Like certain apples for pies may be disappointing, not because you are using the wrong apple, but the apple is out of season and lacks the same quality when it is in season – lost its tart or crispness quality, for instance.

I am curious if foods are still graded. You don't see that any more on packaging. Has it gone out of fashion? Is it necessary? Are we being duped into believing that everything that is sold is "GRADE A" quality foods?

These creeds are priceless. While many people find them antiquated, I believe they are just as relevant today as they were then. Think about it. Whoever is doing the food shopping in the family should take great care in understanding the diet pattern, how to stretch the family food dollar, consider the enjoyment by everyone who will partake in the consumption of the product and understand that this is serious business.

People complain that food is expensive, especially if you want to eat healthy. But the truth of the matter is that food is cheaper than it was decades ago, especially when Meta Given wrote her cookbooks. If you followed Meta's advice, you could stretch the family dollar and save your family a great expense, but not the nutritive value of the food you purchased.

Today it seems that so many people have forgotten and overlooked the importance of their job as the homemaker. We find today that person can be male, female, husband, wife, or whatever your role is. But the seriousness of the role remains the same.

If you are not observing the various pieces of the marketing experience, then you are missing everything. If you ignore the different food groups in your purchase, then it is difficult to have a well-rounded diet. If you do not try to purchase foods that are on sale, in season, then you are overspending and wasting money.

And last, if you do not take into consideration everyone's enjoyment for the consumption of the food, then you may be wasting the purchase of the food. If you buy foods that are not liked then no one will consume them, therefore wasting food and your money. The following creed is as I say just as relevant today as it was some 60 or 70 years hence.

*"The health of my family is in my care"*

The health of one's family cannot be more important than anything else. But we do what is convenient, what will get the job with as little effort as possible. For instance, the outside perimeter of a store is the only place that is dedicated to healthy food. Think about that. Walk up and down the rest of the isles and you will be disappointed when reading the labels of all the prepackaged foods. But those aisles make up most of the store.

*"Stretching the food dollar is part of my responsibility."*

I knew many families who adhered to the "stretching" of the family food dollar. Getting the newspaper was very important; that's where the ads and coupons were every week. Many people only ate that which was on sale. These people only bought things like flour, sugar and other sundries on sale and in bulk.

*"My family's enjoyment of food is my responsibility."*

The person who purchased the food knew everything there was to know about food. The family budget was not taken lightly, and food could be fun at home, like ice cream sundaes or ice cream floats. The budget allowed for picnics, family gatherings and birthday cakes for little parties. All of these things were important for health and wellbeing of the overall family enjoyment.

As important as it was for the breadwinner to go to work, it was also very important for the family homemaker to tend to the proper business at hand of keeping the house in order regarding the purchasing of food and sticking within that all-important budget.

The information that Meta Given accumulated in this chapter and all her chapters had been carefully compiled from a variety of sources, and then she and her staff supplemented the work with their effort to ensure that the information was accurate and relevant.

I believe Meta Given and her staff fulfilled their dream of providing the most up-to-date information in as concise a manner as possible. While this book

# MY TIME WITH META GIVEN

may be 1,700 pages in length, it needed to be to cover so many subjects relating to food. Many cookbooks leave you cold when it comes to the basics. Meta fulfills that hole in her cookbooks.

*"My hope is that it will answer your questions about "stretching the food dollar," about "purchasing fruits and vegetables," about "purchasing staples," such as chocolate, flour, milk, shortenings, sugar, etc., and about "commercially canned foods and their contents."*

This book was not just for the inexperienced cook and homemaker; it was for those with plenty of experience looking for a reference guide as well. The books also were used by colleges, universities and trade schools as classroom books and references. You can find different version of Meta's books in higher education libraries all over the world.

*"It is designed to supplement the knowledge of experienced housewives, to pass on to the new bride the benefit of our experience, and to provide accurate data to all of you who are studying or are just vitally interested in the challenging job of Feeding The Modern Family."*

Homemaker Handbook...Stretching The Food Dollar

The following quote from Meta Given could not be truer today as when it was first written in 1947. This book is still a wonderful resource of information. While you may want to supplement the information, so much of it rings just as true today as it did then. One should always try to stretch their food dollar.

*"Memorize this brief chapter, if you would be known as a good manager! Adopt it as your homemaking creed,*

*and put it into practice every day, for it will help you stretch your food budget so both ends will meet every time."*

So many people complain that healthy food is expensive. This may be true; you can always spend more, but the fun is trying to spend less for high quality food. A bag of apples can cost $5-$10 or they can cost $3. It all depends on how you purchase the apples.

Generally, individual items cost more while buying prepared packages is less. You can purchase a fine quality apple in a bag. However, you can also pay less when they are in season. Not all apples are in season at the same time. So, determine what you need the apples for and purchase accordingly. This will save you money. Also, you can preserve apples when they are in season to be used later for pies, cakes, cookies, breads and such.

Below is some sound advice from Meta that will help you stretch your dollar on a regular basis. You might ask, "What is the point of stretching a dollar?" You might find that economizing will help you save a money, so you don't have to live paycheck to paycheck.

I hear many people complain that there is no way to get ahead. However, I remember living on minimum wage and the things that I did to economize to make the same amount of money go further. Paying less for certain items left me money for saving and emergencies.

Here is the overview of this section: Make it yourself, choose a dependable market, use cash-and-carry service, buy graded merchandise, budget your income, have your own garden, use leftovers, and avoid waste.

I know there is a ton of information in each one of these items. Make it yourself – people may say it is expensive to purchase healthy food, but healthy food is so much less expensive than eating out on all levels. A bag of apples cost about the price of a bag of chips. If you buy the apples in season or in bulk, you can cut the cost many times over.

Here's another tip: choose a dependable market – some stores deal with mostly local fruits, vegetables, and meats if they can. So, if you review the food, you may find that you get a better value from one store than another.

For instance, I won't mention any names, but I know that a large box store that has recently gone into the food business sells many subpar products, like meat for instance. So, you maybe it getting at a cheaper price, but what about the quality of the product?

Tips that relate to cash-and-carry: if you can't afford to buy food, are using credit and not paying, the bill just increased. The overall price of that and any other goods that you buy goes up when using credit. How to reign in your spending may mean using cash for everything you can until you pay off your credit. "Neither a borrower nor a lender be." - *Polonius in Hamlet,* Shakespeare.

Buy graded merchandise – used to be they graded many foods. Today you will not find that so much. As a matter of fact, that is what I am talking about when you choose the market. Some stores sell lower grades of foods, but they don't actually tell you that they are lower grades. They let you guess that by your purchase, then you discover the bad quality, and take your buying ability to a better-quality merchant.

Budget your income – this is a hard one for many people. Some people believe, "I have a credit card; therefore, I have ready money." It is not true. There are limits, and one needs to find a way to live within their means. As mentioned earlier – a cash system is the best for cutting back on spending.

Have a garden – this is pretty hard. It requires work, education and patience. Most of us just don't have the time in our days to put the effort needed into a garden. Then some will say they don't have the space or even a yard. Well, there is container gardening and you can garden inside a home – both will require lighting. Probably not the first choice, but it is an idea.

Leftovers – so many people hate leftovers. Meta had several ideas of how best to use leftovers. I know my mother used this one – clean out the refrigerator meals. We made goulash, macaroni with leftover tomato sauce and leftover hamburger. Many casseroles are better on the second day – make extra and eat it later.

And the last one – avoid waste – that goes hand-in-hand with leftovers. Try not to buy more than you need and make larger batches to have leftovers. Take the leftovers for lunch. Now you have killed two birds with one stone. You not only made dinner, but lunch. I often make a double or triple batch of eggs in the morning and eat them over several days.

This not only saves time, but also saves money. Now instead of cooking every morning, I save my time. If you only fire up the stove once every three or four days, you are saving on your gas or electricity. Yes, I use the microwave to reheat, but the time is minimal compared to the amount of time and resources required to reheat. You say microwaves cost money. That is true, but this is yet another one of Meta's suggestions.

If you save money with all of the things above, eventually, you will be able to afford the utensils needed to make life a little bit easier. If you make all of your lunches for a year you could save approximately $1,000 in your budget. Each one of these savings mentioned above can save hundreds of dollars over time. People don't notice as they spend money, it just goes out of their bank accounts. But if you budget, conserve and look for ways to save, you will find you can also save a bundle of money.

I am not one to talk about budgets, as that concept eludes me. But I do know about only spending with cash, making all of my own meals, having a garden, using leftovers and looking for the best foods at the right time on sale.

The next section is about ascorbic acid - Citrus Fruits and Vegetables - Tomatoes Green and Leafy Vegetables. Below is an interesting read about vitamin C, also called ascorbic acid. Meta tells us about the daily recommended allowance, and how cooking destroys it, yet proper preservation will avoid its destruction.

Meta really gives us all kinds of information to thoroughly cover the subject. You will be hard pressed to find such detailed information in cookbooks today. This is about just one of the vitamins necessary in the daily diet. Meta suggests that you eat a variety of food so that you get all the vitamins and minerals you need through foods.

*"Ascorbic acid (vitamin C) is the most easily destroyed vitamin."* Therefore, take great care in the preservation and cooking of food with vitamin C.

When you think of vitamin A, think of green and yellow vegetables, yellow and yellow-red fruits, eggs and dairy products.

Vitamin A is the opposite of vitamin C, as it is the most stable of the vitamins.

So, when considering your foods, think about the minerals and vitamins that are contained within those foods. Purchasing Meta Given's cookbook can educate you in ways you can only dream about. Today you get a short article here or a little piece of information there.

The forms of information today are herky-jerky and too short to really provide us with in-depth information, yet that is all we rely on. Meta gives us great information to help us understand why we might be lacking in certain vitamins, how to avoid this situation, and what the lack of vitamins cause: diseases.

*"Of all the vitamins, vitamin A is the easiest to obtain, since it is found in fairly large amounts in a wide variety*

*of foods; but in spite of this, an amazing number of people show a clinical sign of vitamin A deficiency-nutritional night blindness. This shows that an unguided choice of foods can easily result in an inadequate diet, even when the proper foods are readily available. This vitamin is fairly stable to all cooking procedures, but since many of the other vitamins are also found in the same foods with vitamin A, the proper cooking of all vegetables and the use of cooking liquid is still just as important."*

In keeping with the next topic, I see articles on the Internet every so often that tell about the best time to buy ... Meta Given believed there was a special time to buy all foods. Eggs are most plentiful in the spring, yet we buy them all year round. Apples have their time depending on the type of apple and so on – yet we buy apples all year long.

Ever notice how the price of some foods are very high but others are reasonable. Well, there are very good reasons: seasons, location and abundance, to name a few. Any one of the above factors can change the price of food in a heartbeat.

For instance, I remember the year tomatoes were having a bad year and they were scarce. Restaurants started charging extra. Some have never changed and charge extra for all kinds of other condiments and the like. Hidden costs are often unnoticed by the consumer. Many times, the waitress specifically asks if you want something additional to what comes with the meal – like a salad or a sauce. It's because that item will cost extra, beefing up the bill, which is good for the restaurant and the waitstaff's pocketbooks. Not so good for your pocketbook.

So next time you go shopping or to a restaurant, see how much cheaper you can obtain the same thing you purchased in the past. When you make a shopping list, check out the store ads and only choose items you know you will consume that are on sale.

I used to date someone who told me they ate only that which was on sale that week. I know that was pretty much true in our family. My Mother was a master at stretching the dollar with all things possible. Meta Given offers pages and pages of money-saving ideas. Literally, pages and pages, which also include the care of the products as well as their purchase. One of her chapters is about buying staples, which include chocolate, fats, flours, leavening, milk, nuts, olives, pickles, sugars, spices, herbs, extracts, vinegars and food coloring.

Who hasn't bought a spice that seems to last forever? Once you buy a staple, they often last a long time. So, buying the right size can be very important. Too large can spoil, too small not enough and expensive. What is the just-right size, Goldilocks?

As Meta said, that which fits in your budget. If you have allotted $100 for your food budget and buying the bulk throws you over, your best decision can be made as follows:

Do you really need that item this trip?

If you need it, will the smaller amount do for a while?

How much do you use the item?

Once you have assessed the situation, you will usually discover the answer that will fit in your budget.

Meta Given talked about this dilemma throughout her writings: about food purchases and about appliances, utensils and all kinds of things relating to the family overall budget.

If you really do not need it, wait. If you want it, wait. If you want it for ease of use or time savings, wait. Do you see a pattern? "Good things come to those who wait (Fane, 2017)."

No one knew this better than Meta Given. She spent over thirty years of her life getting her education. We know that she worked and went to school simultaneously from about 1902-1922. That was twenty years of education where she had to wait to get the money needed to pay for the next semester. The only thing she didn't get was her Ph.D. But as we can tell from her prolific career, she did not need it. She was the "go-to girl" of the 1920s–1950s. Even today, she is still looked to as a resource for special recipes. Pumpkin pie seems to be a favorite, to name one recipe often sought after.

One of the most important pieces of advice Meta gives is the "Care of Food in the Home." You can save a lot of money if food is cared for properly. Improper care can cost you hundreds of dollars every year. In this book, she spent sixteen pages to be exact on the subject. The print is small, and the advice is important. Within this chapter, she gives instructions on the care of a refrigerator and the freezer. The freezers of today are not like those of yesteryear. No longer do we need to defrost.

*Meta Given's Modern Encyclopedia of Cooking* 1952 edition has 403 pages full of advice before we ever see a recipe. Yet there are thousands of recipes. In her *Modern Family* cookbook, the recipes were numbered. There are 1,137 to be exact. While many of the last numbered recipes were more instructions than recipes, there are over one thousand recipes. She did not number the recipes in the *Encyclopedia* like she did the *Family* cookbook.

We discovered that she wrote other books like *Eating for Efficiency* (1930, Evaporated Milk Association). The only two that she continued to publish for about 30 years is the *Family* and the *Encyclopedia* cookbooks.

*Meta Given's Encyclopedia* cookbook has many other instructions that start each chapter and end the book, like: beverages – coffee and tea, bread – yeast and quick breads, cakes, candy, cereals, cheese, eggs, cookies, desserts, fish, game, meat, pastry and pies, poultry, salads, sandwiches, sauces, soups, vegetables, deep-fat frying and steaming.

But let us not forget about the importance of table setting and service, garnishing, picnics and special meals, dishwashing made easier, your kitchen, kitchen equipment, as well as a glossary and an index. Meta Given's cookbooks are educational references and manuals. You will find just about everything you need to know about the basics.

While it may lack the fads of the day, it could get you through just about all you needed to know about food and cooking.

Through the pages of this cookbook and others, you can get the gist of how to cook, save money and still have time for a lazy-day picnic. She provided it all within the pages of her books.

God bless you and keep you, Meta Given.

# Chapter Seven

## Meta Given and the Women of Her Time

*Dedicated to my dear cousin Laura Roix*

WOMEN were sculptors, scientists, computer programmers, home economists, factory workers, farmers, entrepreneurs, switchboard operators, secretaries, teachers, principals, pilots, architects, contractors, plumbers, presidents, accountants, office managers, painters, authors, journalists, and so many other careers. Yet, repeatedly, I hear that women did not have careers and that it was uncommon during Meta Given's time from 1888-1981.

Virginia Penny wrote a book in 1862 called *How women can make money married or single, in all branches of the arts and sciences, professions, trades, agricultural and mechanical pursuits*. The book has had some 36 printings since.

Now here was a woman with some gumption to try and help women who were getting educations. She provided a book that gave a list of jobs, skills needed, if there would be opposition and the like. A very fascinating read and just as relevant today as it was some 156 years past.

I have heard from so many people in my discussions of this book and my subject Meta that women did not work. Yet here are a few statistics that might shock you.

At the turn of the 20th century the 1900 census states that 21.3 percent of all women worked at a job that listed in the census. This number is probably low based on the fact that many women occasionally did their husbands jobs, they were farm hands, took in work at home and a million other jobs that were not listed or considered work.

Of these women only, 5.6 percent of married women worked. However, 66 percent of single women worked from the age of 15. We also know that women worked at much younger ages often starting around 10 or 11 years of age.

Many of the numbers of women who worked for either money or barter were often not accounted for. So we have been able to say things like women did not work around the turn of the 20th century. But this is not true.

While the work women do around the house – taking care of children, cleaning, cooking, tending farm animals and gardens as well as laundry, making cloth and yarn as well was home make clothing, curtains, runs and such. All that work has never accounted for work.

Women were and still are today the first line of our medical health care. Whom among us have not placed a band aid on a wound or administered an aspirin to our fellow family members as mothers. There is a phrase "Doctor Mom" that many of us use without realizing the implications of what that means.

When Meta Given dedicated her book, she dedicated it to twenty-five women. Who are all these women who had careers? Today we are often shut out of many careers so it we are hard-pressed to find twenty-five women doing the same career. STEMS careers for instance have had their doors closed to women in the most recent past.

Today (2018) people say that women do not belong in the kitchen as chefs, yet many women wrote our cookbooks, taught our classes, prepared our meals, and guided us in all things relating to food. As the saying goes – you educate a man – you educate an individual – you educate a woman – you educate the world.

Many people say women do not belong in technology, yet a woman designed the first common business language known as COBOL (Grace Hopper). Women worked on many of the first computers and were leaders in the technology industry. How we know we are not welcome is by the figures. In 1990 35% of all tech jobs were held by women, however by 2013 only 26% are held by women (2015 Huffington post). Obviously, women are no longer welcome in this field.

It is said that women do not belong in the cockpit of an airplane, yet we sacrificed our lives, our families and our souls to fly planes during World War II (go Elizabeth L. Gardner). We were good enough to train pilots, but we were not good enough to "be the pilot."

Women are okay if they are in the service fields - secretaries, waitresses, trainers, teachers, clerks, and your caregivers – you know, your mothers. But we are not okay as your president (Democratic Nominee Hillary Rodham Clinton), as your chief financial officers, or as the chairperson of the board; you prefer that we stay out.

The funniest one that I have heard is that women do not belong in the kitchen. If we do not belong in the kitchen, then how is it that so many mothers are award-winning cooks in their child's eyes?

Why is it that we want the comfort foods that our mothers made - they are women, aren't they? Or did I miss something? I know that my mother is an award-winning chef. She cooks like a professional and always expects perfection in every meal that she concocts.

Meta always made a point for women by saying, "The woman is doing a double job – working outside and cooking for her family at the same time." She was very aware of women who had double the load and how hard it is to make everything from scratch (Given M. , Ration Points Must Have Careful Study If Family Budget Is To Be Maintained, 1943).

Meta gave plenty of advice on how to quicken your process by using the fruits and vegetables that are in season and more plentiful. She also described ways to serve an orange as opposed to buying orange juice to save points and ration your food dollars. Why not just serve either oranges or grapefruit in slices?

I look at the movie *Mr. Mom*, which shows just how marketable a woman can be who has stayed at home. She can relate her personal experience to the job at hand. Yet, when the husband stays home, it takes quite a while for him to manage the household.

The homemaker's skills elude him as his education had not prepared him for the basics, while her skills have been sharply honed while working as a manager of the family household. These skills are easily transferable from in the home and beyond the home (Hughes, 1983)!

I believe that we need to start treating people who manage their homes with the respect that is their due. These acquired skills are transferable to resume items. If you get the education of hard knocks at home, then this becomes a practical education. Why is time spent at home not viable? It is because generally a woman is the one who stays at home. Therefore, it is another way in which to downgrade women. We need to make proper use of this untapped resource.

There is a book out there called *All I Really Need to Know I Learned in Kindergarten* by Robert Fulghum. If that is true, then why do we need college educations?

Many people without college educations have been some of the brightest innovators and inventors in the world. Melanie Klein (by Gail Donaldson, 2017), Nellie Bly (Kroeger, 2013), Steve Jobs (Steve Jobs, 2017), Abraham Lincoln, and the most famous of all Leonardo da Vinci.

These educations are known as autodidactic: self-educated. They believed in themselves and did not give up with a few failures or setbacks. They pursued, they fought, they engaged, they believed in their abilities. They never wavered from what they were trying to accomplish, and they never took no for an answer.

College educations are overblown. If you look at Meta Given, she learned most of what she knew from her mother's elbow. She learned to cook, market, budget, to run a business and she learned so much more. Yes, she went to college, but even she could see that what she learned there was just an extension of what she already knew. The education was giving her confirmation of why. She knew the what, she knew the how, but she did not necessarily know the why (Given M. , Cookbook, 2017).

With her education, she now fully understood why you should cook the cabbage with the cover off the kettle or why puncturing the peel of the beet before you cooked it was not a good thing. Did Meta need her education? She certainly needed to know how to read and write. But she could have done much of what she did without further education. However, her parents believed in education; they both knew how to read and write, which was important in the mid-1800s.

By the time Meta Given was born in 1888, public education was sweeping the nation through required public-school educations, which meant the need for educated teachers. In comes the Normal schools. Meta Given and her sister Carrie were just two of millions of women who obtained that education (Bishop, 2013).

In my research about how many women went to college during the late 1800s and the early 1900s, college educations did not include the Normal education category. By doing this, we downgrade the education level that many women who dominated Normal schools obtained.

Therefore, the number of women who got Normal school education was about 79 percent of the attendees. According to a 1993 study of 120 years of education, 38% of 20-24-year-old women had were enrolled in educational pursuits (Snyder 1993).

Here are just a few women who had careers and excelled with and without educations:

Evelyn Beatrice Longman (Batchelder) (1874-1954) sculptor – first woman to be a member of the National Academy of Design in 1919. She created important sculptures – Victory 1904, Great Bronze Memorial 1909, Wreaths, eagles and inscriptions 1914 on the Lincoln Memorial, Bronze Eagle on the Green in Windsor, CT 1927, to name a few (Evelyn Beatrice Longman, 2013).

Marie Curie (1867-1934) – scientist who won 2 Nobel prizes - Nobel Prize in Physics 1903, 1911 Nobel Prize in Chemistry, also in 1909 the first female professor at University of Paris after her husband's death (Marie Curie, 2017).

Dr. Evelyn G. Halliday (1877-) from Canada – Professor of Home Economics of the University of Chicago for many years and the person who wrote the forward in Meta Given's Cookbook (1917).

Irma Rombauer (1877-1962)– author of *Joy of Cooking* cookbook – wrote and self-published in 1931 on her own and through a publishing house since 1936 continuously (The Joy of Cooking, 2017).

Lily Haxworth Wallace - Rumford Cook Book - Cookbook author, columnist, and teacher (Lily Haxworth Wallace, n.d.).

Here are two of the twenty-five women Meta Given mentioned in her cookbook:

Elma R. Crain worked as a dietician for the Cook County Hospital and assisted with the *Modern Family Cook Book* in 1942 (Given M. , 1942).

Mary Wright worked on the *Modern Family Cook Book* in 1942 and was the first home (economics) advisor for the Cook County Home Bureau (Given M. , Modern Family Cook book, 1942).

Nellie Bly (Elizabeth Cochran Seaman) – reporter for *New York World* newspaper in 1889 (the year after Meta was born) – She worked for Pulitzer himself. She took all the money she had in the world and headed to New York to convince Pulitzer, who had not responded to her letters, to give her a job.

Initially, she lost her nerve, but then she lost her purse and money, so good old human survival took over. She worked for three hours trying to convince his staff that she must meet him. She obtained a job with an advance after meeting with an editor. One of her assignments was a stunt that was her idea to beat the Jules Verne *Around the World in 80 Days*.

She circled the world in 72 days, telling a good yarn of her deeds using trains and steamships. Later, a famed fast train would take its name from Nellie Bly as a response to this stunt (Nellie Bly, 2017) and (LUTES, 2007).

Lillian Valborg Mariea Helander (1899-1973) lived in Connecticut, Rhode Island. Lillian Helander is known for being a designer of jewelry, a silversmith, and world traveler – discovering all the latest techniques. (Lillian Valborg Mariea Helander, 2017).

Mrs. Leonora Z. Meder (1874-1954) admitted to the bar in Kentucky in 1894. She was in the legal profession as well as politics. She was bold and brash. She believed that she was the best man for the job and she was not afraid to say so. In 1919 she ran for mayor of the second largest city in the U.S. – Chicago. As quoted by the *New York Times* she said, "Can you name one of the candidates who has thrown his hat into the ring who is better qualified than I?" She became city commissioner in 1914 through an appointment. Her outspokenness against contraception and abortion was well known. She was also one of the first to say that women belong in the kitchen because they voted as their husbands – Hillary Clinton accused women of the same crime in the 2016 election, which she lost (Her Hat was in the Ring Biography, 2017).

Elvera Norman Rest (1918-2004) worked on the *Meta Given's Encyclopedia of Cooking* cookbook around 1947 putting in over 18 months helping organize and aiding in the rewriting of many sections. Some information obtained from the Social Security Records held in the ancestor.com website (Given M. , 1947).

Bella Abzug_(July 24, 1920 – March 31, 1998) was an attorney and served in the House of Representatives as well as being a women's rights activist along with other social issues. She was part of the same movement as Gloria

Steinem and planned things like the 1977 National Women's Conference, which President Ford initiated, and she worked with President Carter on a commission for women. She is famous for saying "This woman's place is in the House – the House of Representatives" during her 1970 campaign, which she won (Bella Abzug, 2017).

Our next heroin of great import was Florence Ellinwood Allen (1884-1966), none other than the first female judge sitting upon a State Supreme Court in the state of Ohio. She was also the first of two women to sit as a United States Federal Judge.

When she was starting out in her legal profession, she struggled to get experience when she initially opened her practice. Being the clever lass that she was, she volunteered at the Local Aid Society. This association led to her involvement with the Suffragists and women's causes of the day.

As a child her mother gave her the first taste of suffragettes' by taking her to talks by the likes of Susan B. Anthony and Anne Howard Shaw. Through her volunteer work she gained respect from her male colleagues after winning several cases. By 1919, she was able to gain an appointment as the Assistant Prosecuting Attorney for Cleveland's Cuyahoga county.

All encounters were not a bed of roses when dealing with the Democratic Party, specifically Burr Gongwer. She did meet some opposition, which did not stop the approval of her appointment and she again became the first female to hold this position in Ohio. Within this position, she brings her cases before the Grand Jury (Florene Ellinwood Allen, 2017).

The above list of women is just a small subset of women who have worked and had careers over the years. For instance, all the women who worked in the shirtwaist factories, or the yarn factories, or the thread factories, or all the women who were teachers, principals, and other careers they held regarding our school system, and the millions who lost their jobs because they chose to marry and became mothers. The thousands of women who went to work during World War I and World War II and lost their jobs when our men came home from the wars.

Women have had careers for as long as there have been people. There is a claim that prostitution is the oldest profession which I believe is held by women.

Do you think we were shrinking violets in the cave-dwelling days or on the plains of the Savannah in Africa? Notwithstanding in society because we were a threat. That threat has lasted a long time.

It is time that we are seen for who we are, the contributions we make to everyone's lives and the sacrifice we have made for our families, communities, and ourselves.

Meta Given only lived part of the life that women should be allowed to live. She did not marry. Yet she had a very successful career. Was that because she chose not to marry or because marrying was not an option? Married women could not hold teaching positions, and many other jobs fell in with these blatant discriminatory rules.

There was little or no way for her to obtain a job to help supplement her income except for things like seamstress work, taking in boarders in the home, or domestic work, even though she may be college-educated. One such woman did something truly amazing in her day. She wrote and published her own cookbook. Today it is one of the most famous of all cookbooks, the *Joy of Cooking*.

Women were forced out of their careers the moment they married by pre-established rules such as those dictated for school teachers. Companies like Ford Motor Company believed that they paid a man's wage enough to support the family. But, again, there was no consideration given if the man could no longer support his family or was not willing to fulfill his obligations of the day.

With this biography I hope to right a wrong by putting Meta Given back into history where she belongs. Even the *New York Times* is trying to right the wrong of not running obituaries of women through history.

One of the women I mentioned above, Evelyn Beatrice Longman was a sculptor who started her career around the turn of the twentieth century. When Evelyn met her husband, she was about forty years old. She hesitated when asked to marry because of her fear - the fear of not being "allowed" to continue working.

After reassurance from her future husband, Nathan Batchelder, she could continue her work. Nathan, the headmaster at Loomis (Chaffee) School even had a studio at the school built for her. Evelyn then agreed to marry Batchelder. She was one of the lucky few who did not have to give up her career.

Shutting women out of powerful careers kept many gifted women from their career choices – especially in science, mathematics, astronomy and so many others. Women obtained college degrees, but did not necessarily go on to get their master's or Ph.Ds. Even if they did, they were not always allowed to participate at the top levels.

For instance, these astronomers were shut out of the coveted positions. Instead, they more often worked as clerks - they called them computers, doing the drudgery type tasks. However, many women still outshone men with their gifted abilities. For instance, Annie Cannon (1863-1941) was an astronomer who was well educated and very capable. She only achieved assistant to the director of the observatory.

Yet, her diligent work, her negotiation abilities, her organizational skills and so much more helped her become top of her field. She discovered the most number of stars: some 500,000. She also came up with the stellar catalog system. This was in part due to a compromise because two men could not agree on a solution.

Annie Cannon made astronomy what it is today through her writings and negotiations. There are countless women from the late 1800s through the 1900s with similar stories. They were the best in their field, but many times they were held back from being top in their field (Annie Jump Cannon, 2017).

However, there are also many women who did become top in their field despite the times, the circumstances and the many obstacles placed before them.

There are so many notable women that you need a whole library full of books just to cover all their amazing careers. Many of them go into history with little notice - they are the teachers, principals, secretaries, architects, landscapers, contractors, sculptors, riveters, factory workers, chefs, entrepreneurs, of every kind and every job imaginable. These amazing may have lost their jobs once married.

These women were often denied promotions and paid below the going rate of a man because they were women.

Almost always, they were paid well below the current wage that men were paid for the same job and qualifications.

Evelyn Longman was just one such woman. However, she was one of the lucky women where her future husband valued her work and understood her genius and worked with her to ensure that he got what he wanted, and she got what she wanted. It was a marriage made in heaven for Evelyn and for Batchelder.

There were all kinds of beliefs about women and work. There were those who believed that married women should give up their jobs so that men and widows who were self-supporting could have jobs. The editor of the *Lincoln Star*, E. E. Fugate, wrote that even President Roosevelt was trying to help weed out the married women who held jobs. Why should a married woman work when she clearly had support? There were plenty of men and widows who were just as good at the work as the married women, according to an editorial written September 4, 1933 (Fugate, 1933).

While this was the clear thinking of the day, it took away from the individuals who contributed their genius. After all, the next person may be just as capable as the last person, but their contributions might not be the same. For instance, could another person have accomplished the body of work that Evelyn B. Longman (Batchelder) accomplished?

I do not believe so. That's like saying if Steve Jobs was not allowed to do what he did because he married and had children that another person would come along and done the same work as he performed.

That is not true. No two people are interchangeable. It is true that two people can do the same work for a company, but when you are talking about innovations, inventions, and artistic abilities, you cannot interchange one for the other.

You cannot take a Leonardo da Vinci out of the equation and believe that someone else's work is the same as the body of work Leonardo accomplished. You cannot believe that you can take Grace Hopper out of the picture and you still come up with COBOL (the common business language).

Each creative individual is just that. An individual. By not allowing people to flourish in their chosen fields, you deny the world the full picture. You miss out on all the possibilities. That is why when you shut women out of a career, you are closing the door on true creativity. You are only hearing half of the story, seeing half of the picture. You are denying the true beauty of the world.

*It is like a sunset without the sun, a crescent moon on the horizon without the moon.*

Another crime of taking women out of their jobs is that it alters their lives in ways that most people cannot imagine. For instance, women who lost their teaching jobs because they married and had children found it very difficult to go back into the workforce after circumstances changed.

If their husband became ill, died, or ran off leaving the family with no support. The result was often poverty. How different lives could have been if discrimination were eradicated. (By the way not just discrimination of women, but any person who has been discriminated against.)

What a crime of our society for destroying the lives and careers of very capable women because of discrimination and lack of forethought.

Today we have other types of discrimination. While it is illegal to fire a woman from her job because she marries, it is not illegal to completely shut women out of careers. Even with all of the laws we have in place, you cannot force companies to hire an equal number of minorities into a company. No matter how you spin the situation, there are women being shut out of careers every day as we speak.

It's hard to believe, but there are managers in places of authority today who will not hire a woman to do the job no matter what the law says. Many deem women as not qualified, even if she has the same or better credentials than the men who are subsequently hired. They don't believe what they are doing is illegal or wrong. They have no interest in working with women.

After all, women belong at home! The misunderstanding of women does not make it right. Yet the implementation of a human resource department has turned a blind eye to discrimination, allowing management free reign.

I am not sure if Meta Given encountered discrimination in her career. She was let go from not one but two jobs within as many years. However, in the home economic field for packing companies like General Mills and Kraft, as well as magazines like *Better Homes and Gardens* and the *Ladies Home Journal* (Brown, 1949) she was invaluable.

She was a very strong woman with some definite ideas about what she was doing and where she was going. After being let go from not one but two companies – she said I have had enough of working for other people, I can do this on my own. She did it for sixteen years with her Scientific Kitchens. She also had an additional twenty-three years when she maintained her two cookbooks until they went out of publication in 1972. She was eighty-four years young.

For thirty-nine years, she called no man her master in the home economics business she successfully ran by herself. There were no men hired into her business. You might say there was some reverse discrimination there. But men were not interested in the "women's" career of *home economics*.

She, however, must have encountered many men within the food packaging companies.

How about all the appliance and utensil companies that she worked for through "Meta Given's Scientific Kitchen's" business? She is noted as having worked for many of the famous packaging companies (Cam.Cty.Tribune, 1938).

I will never spin Meta Given as being someone she was not. However, based on the facts of her full career this is what I see. I see her as a determined individual who was very capable at what she did. Also, she knew where she was going with her career. Therefore, I see her as an assertive woman who knew how to get things done. She was great at navigating her career in ways that even men envied.

*Home Economics* was her destiny!

She was not afraid of the unknown, for she had nothing to fear, but fear itself. I admire her for her ability to turn her love of food into a career. To take that ability and turn it into one of the most successful careers and businesses of the day.

It was like there was so much work that needed to be done in that area. She could not help herself. She talked to people and they gave her many of her ideas for the next article, the next book and even the next career.

At Facebook, one of the sayings they have on the wall in their company as told to us by Sheryl Sandberg, the COO, "What would you do if you were not afraid?" I don't believe Meta Given knew fear. I don't believe it was something that crossed her mind.

I have heard many women talk about their fears, their insecurities and such, but I don't believe these are things that Meta Given shared. I feel confident she was a full-steam-ahead type of woman who believed in her own abilities.

Meta did her research and told the facts as she saw them for what they were. She had knowledge that many of us possess, but she was not afraid to expand on that knowledge. Then Meta shared that information with anyone who listened and of course anyone who paid for that knowledge.

Being a woman writing this book has opened so much information to me about women and careers. I have been reading about women from all the ages. They have always been very hard-working, innovative, inventive, and downright impromptu when the occasion demanded it. For instance, I am currently reading about the "Women who won the West."

They were women who followed their husbands, their brothers, their fathers and whoever else dragged them along or even may have done the adventure on their own. They wrote letters or journals to tell about their adventures. One woman could go no further. She sat down and refused to go – she even hit her son and stopped talking to her husband for days because she had had enough. Yet she persevered in the end (Reiter, The Old West: The Women, 1978).

Going across the country from the East coast to the West coast was quite the adventure. Just taking a plane ride today is its own adventure but imagine walking or riding in a wagon the whole distance. Oh my, all the meals that had to be prepared – sometimes the men prevented the women from stopping at a nice forest area for wood, so they had to pick up buffalo dung for their fires. You think, "How could the men be so mean?"

Men had only one thing in their minds and they did not care if it was more work for the women. They were crossing the continent and they were doing it today. We will not stop and do something that might make it a little easier for women – oh no. They even spanked their women if they did not comply with the way they wanted it done. They also had them jailed for certain infractions.

Once the women who did go to the West had more freedoms than their counterparts in the East. They were able to establish rules as they saw fit. Men appreciated the single women when they did come West. There was a rush on marriages and it didn't matter their age or even if they had been married before. Men were willing to take any woman who came along.

During a performance, a baby could be heard being born. The miner during the 1840s stopped the performance to marvel at the sound. He was mighty happy to know women were around and enjoyed the comforts that came with them.

Many times, the things that made a home for women when they traveled across the continent had to be left behind, if not when they first started the journey then many times during the journey they unloaded anything that might not be necessary.

They even had to give up their bedding for food for the animals if they used hay or straw in the bedding. It was that or the animals starve, and then how to get the wagon across the land? Everything had to be assessed, reassessed and assessed once again as the situation arose. Every woman had her own cross to bear – whether it was the women who came across the Atlantic to the colonies or the women who traveled to the West of the continent (Reiter, THE OLD WEST: THE WOMEN, 1978).

Women have been heroic and have made a difference in history since history began. We just have not shared in the glory of having our names remembered or the deeds that we did recorded. Many times, we were blatantly left out, other times we were omitted because no one spoke up for us. Sometimes they outright stole our ideas, inventions, and discoveries. For the most part we were just plain ignored.

In my search for women in history, I have found so many names of women who silently or not so silently made history. Whether it was with their own family or on the pages of our newspapers, it was seldom in our history books.

Women's stories are out there. There are hundreds of people working every day to put women's names back into our history. There are individuals like Rebeca Swaby with *Headstrong 52 women...* (Swaby, 2015), or major corporations like TimeLife books who did *The Women* book as part of their *The Old West* collection.

So, with this book about Meta Hortense Given, I hope I have added one more woman's name to the annals of history of a woman who "tried to feed a nation." A woman who was the "go-to-girl" of the packing industry, the food photo industry, the newspaper industry and even the magazine industry.

Meta Given deserves her rightful place in our history as one of the most influential *home economists* of her time. She deserves her rightful place in history as the author of not one but two of the bestselling cookbooks of her time. That time was from 1902 - 1972, leaving us with about four million copies of her works of art.

Meta Given deserves her rightful place in history as a food editor and newspaper columnist for her syndicated column that splashed over the pages of newspapers all over this nation reaching some 60 million Americans at the height of her career.

Please welcome our little Meta Hortense Given with an award for being the best of the best in her field from 1902 through 1972. Seventy years of teaching, demonstrating, writing, photographing, cooking and scientifically testing every food of her time to make this nation healthier and stronger.

Meta Given was not a queen, but she wore her crown proudly as the home economist of her day. Meta Given will never show up in a history book, but she altered history forever when it came to her contributions for the soldiers during not one but two World Wars, with her victory gardens and her writings throughout.

Meta did not toil like those who crossed the continent during the emigration from East to West in this country, but she provided a cookbook that stands the test of time. Meta Given was not the first cookbook author in this country, nor were her cookbooks the last, but they have had a lasting effect on millions just the same.

Meta Given came from a large family of men and women who came to this country from other country. She came from a long line of people who worked hard and were modest and humble about their gifts that they brought with them and passed on from one generation to another. While Meta Given may not have had children to pass her legacy on – she passed it on to one of the largest generations of our times, 70 million strong – Baby Boomers through the Greatest Generation!

In my search for Meta Given and the search of millions of women just like her, I hope we do her the justice that is her due. I believe she was humble in her endeavors of her seventy-year career. But one does not spend seventy years for naught. She might not like the attention or the accolades.

Yet she might like to know that her books and her career touched so many lives and that we still seek her advice as if she were the current chef celebrity.

Thank you Meta Given for saving our families from malnutrition when we needed it most. Thank you for writing not one but two lasting legacies that we can hold in our hands and read your wise words that hold as true today as they did when they were first being written. Thank you, from the bottom of my heart.

Yours truly,

Danette Lynn Bishop Mondou!

P.S. Thanks Mom, for purchasing and your guidance and cooking lessons from Meta Given (*Encyclopedia of Cooking* 1953).

# Chapter Eight

## Meta's Life and Times

*Dedicated to my grandmother Hazel Gerow, I know you did the best you could with what you had!*

IT is always neat to go back into history and find out what was going on when we were born. This chapter is exploring just such events for the year that Meta Given was born.

Meta was born in the longest Roman numeral year, with thirteen letters: MDCCCLXXXVIII only to be topped again in the year 2888 some 1000 years in the future. Numbers are neat and adding in the Roman numeral factor increases the fun.

Looking back at the year 1888, there were some interesting events that shaped Meta's life and put into perspective how she took her place within the world that surrounded her at the time.

The wax drinking straw was patented on January 3 by Marvin C. Stone in Washington D.C. I still remember the wax straw; today they are all plastic. You don't think that something so minute could affect the world so dramatically, but I think of my daughter and how much easier it was to wean her from the baby bottle with the straw, and the sippy cup was a cup with a built-in straw. How far we have come (Thompson, 2011).

The centimeter or refracting telescope located in California was used for the first time in the Lick Observatory on January 3, just twenty-two days before Meta's birth. Imagine the whole new worlds that the telescope opened for all of us. It was the largest in its time and currently is the third-largest telescope at this writing (1888, 2017).

At least twenty major discoveries were attributed to this telescope over the years; Double and triple stars once thought to be single stars, accurate positions of comets, as well as stars and planets, to name a few. The technology and all the wonders of nebula that this telescope has discovered are amazing. In Meta's time, not only did we have more powerful telescopes, we traveled into outer space and landed a man on the moon (James Lick Telescope, 2017).

Can we ever forget the adventures of Sherlock Holmes that all began on January 7 with the *Valley of Fear*? While I have never read any of the books, I have watched different shows and there are many references to his writings in popular culture.

The creation of the National Geographical Society in Washington D.C. occurred on January 13, just twelve days before Meta was born. This society is the largest in the world for nonprofits interested in geography, science and archaeology. I wonder if Meta ever requested an invitation to join the Society. It was a big deal to be invited to be a member back in the day.

Also, in Washington D.C. Susan B. Anthony's organization of the Congress of Women's Rights (The National Council of Women of the United States) was created in 1888 (2017). Susan B. Anthony was very important in women's rights and the women's voting amendment. Her life did not directly intertwine with Meta's, but Susan helped Meta without ever knowing the impact she had on Meta and millions of women who have come after (1888).

Two interesting things that advanced women's careers occurred in 1888: the first was the method of typing called "touch typing" that won the contest for fastest typing on July 25 and Gregg Shorthand was published in the U.S. on December 23. Both skills were in great demand in the next century and women dominated the field known for years as secretarial. I wonder whether Meta used a typewriter to write her books and articles or if she used a good old pen and paper. Not something I am ever likely to discover.

Recently, I went to the Mark Twain (1835-1910) house built in 1874 in Hartford, Connecticut. It is a beautiful home with some very neat and unique features.

On the third floor is a pool table with notecards that Mark used to prepare for his speeches and write his books. There was a typewriter, not something he used much, but it was the up-and-coming tool of the trade for writers. It would be nice to see a room like that of Meta Given's life if such a thing still existed.

With electricity came many inventions, such as the first electric railway system used in the streets of Richmond, Virginia, as early as February 2 invented by Frank Sprague, also known as the "Father of Electric Traction." His inventions and ideas also included elevators, railways and motors. Think of how much we take advantage of these inventions (Frank Julian Sprague, 2017).

While golf has been played since the middle ages in Scotland and they formulated the eighteen-hole course and rules, it would not be until 1888 on February 22 that John Reid of Scotland would demonstrate this game in Yonkers, New York. I have read recently that the millennial generation is not interested in the sport. What is to become of the game in this country?

There seems to be some discrepancy as to when the first secret ballot was used in this country, according to the site that I obtained this information from originally. However, from the wiki page, the dates are all around the late 1800s from 1890, when most states printed the secret ballot known as the Australian and later as the Massachusetts ballot (Secret Ballot, 2017).

On February 24, Louisville, Kentucky became the first government in the U.S. to adopt the Australian ballot (i.e., secret ballot on standard voting forms).

Then there was Thomas Edison (1847-1931) of light bulb fame (1879). He talked of motion pictures, film with sound on February 27 in 1888. Electricity was something that Meta embraced as she advanced in her life. It was probably not something she used as a young girl, but something she included in her career during her testing of the latest appliances for the kitchen (Thomas Edison, 2017).

On March 6 Louisa May Alcott, the prolific writer of the mid to late 1800s who wrote *Little Women* (1868), died of a stroke at the age of 55 years old in 1888. She grew up amongst the likes of Ralph Waldo Emerson, Nathaniel Hawthorne and Henry David Thoreau. She was one of many women who were educated yet had to help her family financially.

She began writing at an early age with the pen name A.M. Barnard. Louisa was one of our suffragettes and an abolitionist who did not marry in her lifetime. She lived in the Concord and Boston Massachusetts areas (Louisa May Alcott, 2017).

The year 1888 brought some horrific snowstorms. Storms that become benchmarks for all future storms, even in the twenty-first century. The first would be the Schoolhouse Blizzard (Schoolhouse Blizzard 1888, 2017) that would blanket the plains of the Midwest in January before Meta was born. Then the Great Blizzard of '88 would strike the East Coast and Canada from March 11-14. These storms would leave their area devastated for days, killing over 230 people, mostly children, in the Midwest region and over 500 people in the northeast coastal area (Great Blizzard of 1888, 2017).

One crazy event was the feat of moving the Brighton Beach Hotel on April 2 through the 11 located on Brighton Beach near Coney Island as it was moved some 490-520 feet away from the ocean to protect it from destructive storms. Eventually, the Brighton Beach Hotel succumbed to its demise and now is only a distant memory (Brighton Beach, 2017).

There were several large buildings that were completed in 1888, such as the Texas State Capital building in Austin on April 21 for $3 million, and the Washington Monument was completed on the 9th of October.

Besides Meta Given being born in 1888, so were these other very notable people: Irving Berlin the composer was born on May 11, and Jim Thorpe claims he was born on May 28. He became a professional football player as well as played many other sports in college. However, his baptismal papers say May of 1887, not 1888. I often find these discrepancies in history make life a little more intriguing, and when people talk about fact-checking – well, that is subjective really (1888, 1888).

On May 21 May Aufder Heide was born in 1888. She was a ragtime composer, one the most famous of her time, composing many of the more popular tunes of the day. She went on to compose and publish *Richmond Rag, The Thriller, Buzzer Rag, Blue Ribbon Rag, A Totally Different Rag, Novelty Rag, and Dusty Rag*, plus a number of waltzes and other songs, including *I'll Pledge My Heart To You*, and a song version of *A Totally Different Rag* with lyrics by Earle C. Jones (May Aufderheide, 2017).

I can read the headline now: Leroy Buffington obtains patent for skyscrapers to pollute our skylines. In 1881 he claimed to have thought up the idea of building skyscrapers by using load-bearing iron frames. He applied for a patent in November 1887 and received it in May 1888. Even though many subsequent builders used this method of construction, Buffington was mostly unsuccessful in collecting royalties from his patent (one exception was for the Rand Tower in Minneapolis). Buffington remained in private practice in Minneapolis until his death on February 15, 1931 (Leroy Buffington, 2017).

Some of Buffington's works include:
Pillsbury A-Mill (1881), Main Street and 3rd Avenue Southeast, Minneapolis (National Historic Landmark)
National/Mammoth Hotel (1893, demolished 1936), Yellowstone National Park

After 1880, most seismometers were descended from those developed by the team of John Milne, James Alfred Ewing and Thomas Gray, who worked as oyatoi gaikokujin in Japan from 1880 to 1895. These seismometers used damped horizontal pendulums. Seismographs have a very, very long history, but the one obtained in California on June 1 in 1888 would be the one developed by Milne, Ewing and Gray in the 1880s (Seismometer, 2017).

On June 3 *Casey at the Bat* was published. *Casey at the Bat: A Ballad of the Republic* Sung in the Year 1888 is a baseball poem written in 1888 by Ernest Thayer. First published in *The San Francisco Examiner* (then called *The Daily Examiner*) on June 3, 1888, it was later popularized by DeWolf Hopper in many vaudeville performances. It has become one of the best-known poems in American literature (Casey at the Bat, 2017).

On June 23, Frederick Douglass was the first African American nominated for President. While he was a supporter of the female suffrage movement, he did not support their emancipation at the same time as black men. (Frederick Douglass, 2017).

Then on June 27, Antoinette Perry was born. She was the New York Stage Director who was the namesake for the Tony Award. She had a short-lived career as an actress, however, she was influential as she co-founded the American Theater Wing.

We have Joseph P. Kennedy born on December 6. He was not only a politician, but he became the father of the 35th President of the United States, John F. Kennedy. He also was the father of Robert, Joseph, Teddy, and Eunice Kennedy Shriver.

T.S. Eliot the writer and Nobel Prize Laureate was born on September 26, Eugene O'Neill also a writer and Nobel prize winner, as well as Dale Carnegie were born in November. Carnegie becomes a world-renowned writer and lecturer on *How to Win Friends and Influence People.*

On December 23, just days before Christmas, Vincent van Gogh cut off his ear (ouch). A couple of months before that, the first motion picture of two seconds, lasting for eighteen frames was made, right after that George Eastman registered a patent for the first camera which used roll film for the Eastman Kodak Trademark. Eastman Kodak, founded by George Eastman patented the Kodak box camera on May 7 (George Eastman Patents, 2017).

Lest we forget, the Rescue of the Renown was off the shores of the Netherlands by DORUS Rijkers in March.

Brazil abolished slavery, the Long Indian Reservation at Fort Belknap was established, and Anne Besant organized the London Match Girl Strike as Jack the Ripper caused all kinds of havoc all over London with his killing of several women.

So many interesting and intriguing events shape the world as we knew it then at the end of the 1800s. One of those forces to be reckoned with was Meta Hortense Given.

# Chapter Nine

## What about women, where did Meta fit in?

*Dedicated to the Next Generation of Women*

Meta Given taught hundreds of students in a twenty-year teaching career, then she went on to mentor many young women in the career of home economics as they graduated from the University of Chicago, while supporting herself with an experimental scientific kitchen business. Meta maintained a staff of three or four people over the life of her business for sixteen years.

During the tenure of her business, she single-handedly provided scientific knowledge to a nation literally starving for better, cheaper foods. She provided ways to enhance economical meals that were nutritionally well-balanced.

She started her column of how to "Feed a Family of Four on $10 a week" articles once she learned that young men were starving and unable to join the armed forces during World War II because of poor health. Sometimes the dollar amounts were different. All of her articles were based on the theme that you could feed your family of four economically with the highest quality of nutrition. These articles became a syndicated column and were published in newspapers throughout the United States.

While Meta Given was growing into a young lady the country was going through the Gilded Age. Mark Twain coined the phrase in 1873, in *The Gilded Age: A Tale of Today*. We had such opulence as the building of mansions in Newport, Rhode Island. We also had some of the worst poverty the world has ever seen (Twain, 2017).

The Gilded Age coincided with the Industrial Revolution and the increase in wages despite the influx of immigrants and the ever-increasing workforce. Meta benefited from these inventions in her domestic life and in her career.

She did not marry, which helped her maintain her career especially as a school teacher.

Many business owners also believed that women should not work, as married women took jobs away from men, "the breadwinners." Business owners such as Henry Ford believed that he provided a living wage for his workers, and it was his habit to inspect homes to ensure that they were living to the standard that he believed they should live by (Ford, 1924).

One small flaw in the belief that married women should not work was that what happened when the husband was no longer able to provide, such as through illness, absence or death.

A married woman or widow often found themselves in need of work. Many were left to taking in boarders, doing laundry, or mending when they could have used their educations to continue working as teachers, scientists, secretaries and many other better-paying jobs.

The author of the *Joy of Cooking* cookbook published her own cookbook after her husband died. The cookbook is still in print today and managed by her descendants. Not all women were as lucky (History Joy Cooking, 2017).

The 1800s was a progressive century, seeing great strides in philosophy, mathematics, science, and technology. It was a wonderful time for women as they obtained educations, which led to better career opportunities. However, it was also a very trying time for women who felt the continued struggle for equality. Women did not have the right to vote, some could not possess property, and there was the issue of married women losing their jobs because of the double standard.

Women were slaves either to their husband, father, or the oldest male in the family. Many women were told what to do regarding education, how to dress and whom they could associate with outside the home. Even when given money and property after the death of their family through wills or dowries, they could not possess this inheritance themselves. If they were married, the husband controlled the property to spend as they choose. (Hickox)

In 1919, when Al Capone took over Chicago as the mob boss, Meta Given was still at the University of Chicago. I can't even imagine what must have been going through people's minds with that kind of activity going on in your own backyard. The most notorious gangster was shooting up the streets of Chicago and you are trying to concentrate on your college studies.

So many wonderful, horrible and incredible things happened from the time Meta Given was born until she died. She lived a long and illustrious life from 1888 to 1981, ninety-three years. We go from the Civil War's aftereffects, the Industrial Age, the Gilded Age, straight into the Information Age through two world wars, the Spanish American war, the Cold War, the Korean War and the Vietnam War.

We have the cooking revolution, which saw over a thousand cookbooks being published in the 1800s. The most important books were written by Amelia Simmons an orphan who was illiterate, and the wonderful cooking abilities of Fannie Farmer who brought the Industrial Age to cooking.

Then we have important scientists like Meta Given who was a home economist through her scientific knowledge about food, nutrients, measurements and all the inventions one could throw at you in one century. She made the most of her knowledge in her daily consulting business. She was the one everyone went to for the knowledge of the day regarding these all-important subjects – nutrition, diet, scientific intricacies of food, as well as photography and the testing of various appliances like refrigerators.

What happened to Meta Given? Where did she go? Why isn't she part of history, or should I say (her)story? So much has been left out of the rich herstory and the significant contributions women have made every step of the way.

We know very little of all that women did. The entire history and importance of home economics has been wiped off the face of the planet. It was considered a woman's career and of little consequence, therefore it is of no consequence. Yet that revolution made us healthier, helped us be better parents, helped us provide food at low cost with the highest nutrition and gave us some of the best diets available.

There are many important women who helped the nation with their education in the home health sciences which would be known as Home ec. to many of us in the modern 20th century. The Beecher sister, Ellen Swallow Richards (MIT Chemistry) and of course Meta Given just to name a few were instrumental in starting, organizing, and furthering the science for the better of humanity.

Home economics started out to help farm women as their husbands learned about agriculture, they would learn about home sciences. This grew to organizations like the granges which were buildings were women would gather to learn about the latest in child care, sanitation, kitchen setup, food nutrition and so many other subjects under the home ec. umbrella.

Today we have might be considered a "charismatic celebrity" such as Martha Stewart who is making a small fortune off of home economic themes. She sells it all. I just watched her in an interview and she talked about how she tried to put herself in the place of the consumer to try and provide products and services that she would like to have. It most definitely works for her.

The 1900s find us giving up our horse-drawn carriages and wagons. During this time, we start using plastic for more and more products. And we also transform from working with our hands to using one machine or tool to get the same thing accomplished with less labor and far less time.

It was thought that women should stay in the home and be wives, but many women did not want that path for their lives. At least not at a young age. Women wanted to acquire educations and jobs.

They wanted to see the world. Then if they wanted to get married women wanted that as an option, not as a must. Why even Gloria Steinem would get married at 66 one of our heroic feminists of the late 20th century.

The late 1800s gave women careers like no other time in history. We could finally work outside of the home as the "rules" lifted on that injustice. Women provided cheap labor. They were willing to work for less. So why shouldn't men seek out women to do the work that men could not afford to do with a family?

Many professions paid women differently than men. Schoolteachers were one of these professions that paid different wages for men and women even with the same education and qualifications.

Often if a principal job was available men were offered the job even right out of school, yet women were seldom offered that opportunity. Women's wages were half or less than men for the same teaching position with the same education. Yet women made up 79 percent of the students at Normal schools.

Women could work at many jobs if they did not marry or get pregnant. But men could work regardless of their married situations and were often encouraged to get married. Once a woman became a wife she often lost all her rights as a human being.

Married women were not allowed to possess property, money, enter into contracts and so many other rights were denied them. Trapped chattel of their husband's mercy or merciless as the case might be. Even if left property and money by their families, that property was handed over to the husband to do with as they choose (Hickox, 1871).

I can see why many women chose educations and jobs over marriage. Women by the thousands were getting educations through the Normal School system that was put into place starting in the 1800s and became a sweeping trend by the end of the 1800s.

With these educations, they could get jobs that may not have paid exceptional wages but offers a way out of the marriage options. It also gave them work that saved them from the factories where many women went who could not obtain educations.

Factories were jobs that were offered to women in the thousands throughout the nation, making all kinds of goods and products. With the 1800s came the industrial revolution.

With that revolution came factories that perfected the manufacturing of all kinds of goods. Clothes off the rack, utensils, phone operators, typists, secretaries and so many other careers based on manufacturing.

People like Elizabeth Cochran Seaman aka Nellie Bly, Henry Ford, and Thomas Edison employed thousands of people in factories. They provided every type of job imagined at their factories.

Everyone needed cheap labor, and cheap labor was easily had at the turn of the century. The country swelled with immigrants. They came by the boatloads and they learned to read and write English through the school system.

From there they got jobs. Many women turned to writing. It was a way to obtain a job without the normal constraints and rules that teaching may have had. Home economics was a new career path dominated by women. There were so many directions you could go within that field.

There was another avenue for women and that was charity work or women's organization. With the educations women obtained, they were better able to organize. And organize they did until they got the right to vote in 1920. They also used their charity work to build schools, churches and hospitals.

Many of these organization raised the funds for their own projects through garden clubs, book clubs, with many of them coming from church groups originally starting in the Progressive era in the late 1800s. (Various, 2018)

Meta Given goes in several directions within her lifetime. First as a school teacher, then as a nutritionist and dietitian as the Director of the home economics department at the Evaporated Milk Association. She scientifically tested all kinds of foods and dishes to encourage the public to purchase evaporated milk as an alternative to milk (Introducing New Members, 1925).

From there she became a home economics Journalist Food Editor. In this job, she spends much time scientifically testing recipes, talking about food and diet, and conveying that information in a journalistic with daily articles. She works for none other than the *Chicago Tribune* (Given M. , Food Talk, 1930 - 1931).

She takes all that she knew and became an entrepreneur working for all the large packaging companies as well as many manufacturers and even book publishers. Meta Given was a chameleon when it came to home economics. She sees opportunities that were profitable. While she may not have looked at the results in that light, I am sure based on her personality and style she saw issues, then she came up with solutions. Those solutions just happened to be money-making ideas.

Meta Given became many things to many companies and people. To her, she was just doing the right thing at the right time. Writing about her passion, food, was nothing more than a solution to help the American people when they needed it most with the products that were at hand.

There were many women who did just as Meta did, starting around the turn of the nineteenth century. With the invention of home economics, there were many women standing in line to create the scientific branch. There were many women willing to take up the cause as they saw their skills lending a hand in the fight for what women needed because of the poverty that occurred with immigration.

These women were never ending. There were hundreds of thousands of women who were home economists. Many of them are forgotten as time has passed by. We can find many of them through school rosters, through books they wrote, and through schools they attended. Through education documentation where they taught. We can also find them through the organizations they belonged to or the companies they worked for over time.

They wrote articles in our newspapers across the nation. If you look at the newspapers, there were pages they called "Women's Pages." Those pages were loaded with articles written by women in all kinds of subjects relating to home economics. Articles about food, clothing, babies, exercise, family advice, how to knit, how to sew, how to dress, how to act and so much more.

There were other pages that provided education such as math, history, science and many other subjects. Papers were full of useful information. Many of these articles were written by women who did not get credit for their work.

Meta Given wrote for the *Chicago Tribune* under the title "Food Talk." Six other women wrote this article. Caroline S. Maddox, whose pen name was Jane Eddington wrote the article for about 30 years until she retired. Meta Given wrote the column from June of 1930 until about July of 1931. Then about five women using the pen name Mary Meade wrote the article. The most famous of the Mary Meade author/food editors was Ruth Ellen Church. Ruth wrote it the longest, from sometime in the 1930s until the 1970s. I found it interesting that the article did not include Meta Given. She was the only one who did not use a pen name (Eddy, 1997).

The 1800s started the women's revolution. It truly did something that no other time had done. Women as a mass group got educations and as a consequence, came jobs. Not just a few women but thousands of women. Then there were many wars that taught us that women were truly valuable work resources. It took World War II to finally give women the right to have jobs, keep jobs and not always get fired from their jobs because they were married, or a man might be waiting in the wings.

The only problem is that the beliefs and customs have still not been changed. We still live by the same rules. Women do not need to make as much money as men. If a woman is doing a job that can make a lot of money, men start to dominate the job. It is only worthwhile to them if it is a big money-maker. And they (men) are ruthless in cutting women out and stealing their ideas.

I just watched a documentary called *MissRepresented* where it documented why we keep being put in our place. The government, advertisers and businesses were worried that women were getting too many rights and taking too many jobs after WWII. They conspired to keep women in their place by seducing us with luxury goods for the household, clothing and lots of other junk.

Looks like we bought it hook line and sinker, because through the 1950s more women stayed home than worked. However, come the 1960 and the 1970s women progressively took jobs. We even started getting STEMS jobs where the money is. Guess what ladies, they started another campaign in the 1980s and 90s which have has losing out on the lucrative jobs.

Case in point with journalism, chefs and technology. All careers that were dominated by women at one point in the twentieth century. However, with subtle changes by men, these jobs have all been taken over by men. For instance, women dominated the food editors jobs. Specifically, Jane Nickerson was the food editor for the *New York Times*. When she left, a man took over the job. His statement was that it was time that a man had the job. Really, what did he know about being a food editor? As it turned out, he changed the job from something that was beneficial to our society as a whole into something that was a joke and a way to get free meals at restaurants.

Many careers were stolen from women. We have stood by while men have taken our jobs, gotten paid better and scorned us when we try to get jobs in the careers that we made famous in the first place. For instance, it was women who were the first software developers. Can we ever forget the indelible Grace Hopper? The mother of COBOL. Yet men will tell you that we don't belong in this field. They pushed us out of the technology field, even though we dominated the field at its birth. Initially, a computer was a human, and generally the job was held by a woman. It has become a very high-paying field in all branches, and they want us out.

Meta Given was a scientist. She dominated her field in the 1900s from about 1925-1950. Yet do we see her name anywhere in reference to the history of home economics? Nope. I have done much research and she is just not mentioned. There are books and articles aplenty, but no mention of one of the most important home economists of our times. Why can I make such a claim? Because it is true (Sara Stage, 1997).

If we can make people today famous for nothing, then we should make Meta Given famous for something. She fed a nation when the nation needed strong and healthy individuals to go to war, work in our factories, and to cook our meals. The work and research that Meta Given did from 1902 until 1972 has not been forgotten by those of us who appreciated the home-cooked meals.

We would not be as healthy as we are today, if not for the basic principles that we take for granted, such as washing our hands often and frequently. Clean drinking water (Richards late 1800s), toilets in our home. Women brought those innovations into our homes through their scientific research, perseverance and determination no matter the road blocks placed before them (Swaby, 2015).

Meta was no different than Ellen Swallow Richards, Fannie Farmer, Catherine and Harriet Beecher Stowe. Many women worked tirelessly towards the health and welfare of the people of this country (Feeding America, 2013). Meta Given was just one such woman. Her contributions were all about food.

She tested, retested and tested again every aspect of food. She didn't believe her contributions were all that great (Nickerson, Cooking Encyclopedia Author Full of Information, 1975). But if you review the information about her life, the facts tell a far different story. That is of all the amazing things she accomplished. We found a woman dedicated to bringing the American family healthy wholesome food at an economical price.

There are many aspects of home economics. Meta actually dealt with two of them specifically: food and finances. While she did not teach finances directly, she encouraged the caregivers of this nation time and again to economize with each meal so that you could occasionally enjoy the finer things in life.

Ellen Swallow Richards is noted as the first woman accepted to a school of science and technology. Her degree of choice was chemistry. Her school choice which had its limitations in 1860s and 1870s was Vassar College. Mrs. Richards' many contributions to the world including home economics, school lunch and euthenics (Ellen Swallow Richards, 2017).

The Department of Domestic Economy at Washington State (WSU) was established in 1903. It emphasized the basic sciences as well as classes in sewing and millinery, cooking, and household economy and management. In order to graduate with a home economics degree, students studied fine arts, chemistry, and bacteriology. They learned human nutrition, accounting, teaching, food preparation, culture, and early childhood development.

In 1913, Washington State University's extension program hired its first home economist, whose job it was to take the expertise of home economics to the rural residents of the state. One of the earliest interior design projects at WSU that was later applied to homes in the region had to do with optimum counter heights in a working farm kitchen (Sudermann, 2017).

Stretching the dollar was also an early consideration. In 1918, one student wrote her master's thesis on furnishing a home for a family of five on an income of $1,500 a year. During the Depression, Washington State's students focused on projects like turning flour sacks into clothes and making their own mattresses.

We had fewer heart attacks, and diabetes was not a major issue, like it is today. We may have had cancer, but not to the degree we have it today. Companies looked for the best nutrition, not just the cheapest way in which to manufacture their product. They enhance food with nutrients. Unfortunately, they were processing nutrition out of our food one process at a time as early as the late 1860s, and eventually have done everything they can to make food as tasty and addicting as possible with little or no regard for the nutritional value.

We need to go back in time with the new knowledge of today and marry the old with the new so that we come up with the latest and the greatest at a price that everyone can afford, which includes the natural remedies for certain diseases that have been tried and true. Unfortunately, we have something called the FDA, which prevents us from common sense solutions.

We often overlook the simplicity of life. People complain about the cost of items, but really, they don't cost that much more than they did twenty, thirty or even a hundred years ago. We just have gotten lazy and we expect more, and we want less work time and more leisure time. The funny thing is the things we want to do in our leisure time don't really satisfy us like cooking a wholesome meal or making our own quilts or designing something for practical purposes.

We do many useless things with our lives instead of teaching our children to be better citizens of the world. Many men play sports excluding women from the game. Continually, teaching children that we are separate and not equal by putting more emphases on male sports than women sports.

Where we should be putting equal emphases on both sexes and making sure that society understand that women are an integral part of their world to be treated like people. And to educate our women that they are important, their opinions matter and giving them an equal share of educations by calling on them in class.

I often think of the young man who went into the wild and had no life skills from his childhood to draw upon. When I was a child, I learned all about the practical gathering of fruit, berries, and other natural foods. I also learned how to make nutritious meals from scratch economically.

This young man knew nothing about that. He could not tell the difference between berries, or how much meat he needed for himself. He was very impractical in his understanding of the knowledge that should have been passed down from generation to generation (Krakauer, 2007).

I feel so fortunate that I have this basic knowledge, but most people struggle when they try to live on minimum wage, when they know nothing about the concept of making meals from scratch or going into the wild to forage for food. We need to bring these skills back. We need to make them mainstream.

Meta Given was perfect for helping us forage for food, gather the food, process the food and combine the food into meals that are savory and sensory as well as economical.

I believe we should each create something unique at our own homes. We should look at what we can do. I know that I have learned how to do so many things. Meta Given was just such a person. She grew up on a farm. She lived with a woman who took in boarders.

She lived in apartments where she got to know her neighbors. She also owned her own home where her mother lived with her, she took in boarders and she even did charity when she rented out her garage to a family who needed a little help.

The father built a floor from materials he found in the neighborhood. Making the garage livable. Today, no one thinks of living in a garage. It is great shelter and with proper care, it can be made into livable space. Many families that are down and out on their luck only need a little leg up. This helped them get back on their feet.

These are the lessons we learn from Meta Hortense Given. She started out with nothing. She built a life with her knowledge gathered from her family, from neighbors, from boarding moms, from teachers, and anyone else who was willing to pass on their knowledge.

We've come a long way baby from 1888 until 2018 and beyond. Yet we are not doing as well as we could economically in the lower and middle classes. I started out with nothing, but I have built a life that is economical. I try to live within my means through my own education and supplemental institutional education.

In 1888, the home economic movement was in full swing with women all over the nation and even the world clamoring for ways to make their lives better, their children healthier with knowledge at their fingertips.

We have gone right into the data age with the help of women like Meta Given born in 1888, who working tirelessly for more than 70 years. Those born in the 1800s have taught us well, we just need to keep passing those lessons on to the next generation.

# Chapter Ten

# Meta Given's Dominance with Women, 1925-1949

*Dedicated to women who dominate their field of choice!*

META Given wrote about so many things in her seventy-year work history. Many of them will be lost forever, and others fill newspapers and cookbooks that she wrote for us to share. It has been my honor and privilege to write her biography. I would like to share some of my favorite newspaper articles that she wrote over her career in this chapter.

I hope to capture her spirit through these articles. There are bits about her family, and even wonderful little tidbits that reflect her personality. She was a humble woman who shared herself through these articles to try and convince the public that spinach was more than an obligation, it could be delicious. She helped us realize that it was more than just something we had to do but something we could enjoy to its fullest once we learned how to cook, season and prepare as never before experienced.

1920s Early Writings

In 1925, Meta Given wrote articles about food:

September 1, she wrote *Drink Milk if You Want to be Beautiful,* an article that was in the *Chillicothe Missouri Tribune* newspaper. This was a dictum by Meta Given, who was still a student at the University of Chicago and the Directory of the Evaporated Milk Association.

I love how the article uses the word "dictum." Meta Given was considered the authority on food in every article that I have read about her. Every article pronounced Meta Given as the most authoritative source of the day.

September 4, she wrote an interesting article about camps title *Girls' Camp demonstrates Healthy Body Creates Healthy Mind*. Meta talked about all the benefits of this "new idea a few years ago" and states that girls camps "have doubled in numbers in the last two years." She talked about how busy they are at camp and lists some of their "diversified subjects such as swimming, needlework and languages" to name a few.

Meta pointed out that dieticians help create a "healthfully balanced diet" consisting of "pure milk, whole cereals, eggs, fresh fruits and vegetables." She wrote, "concentrated food is necessary" as children find it hard to consume enough food to keep up with "their rapid growth." Meta mentioned evaporated milk in this article, which ties in to her career as she is working for the Evaporated Milk Association. She told us that "Bulky menus are taboo. Eggs and nuts and other substitutes are used several times a week in place of meat. Fresh fruits serve as sweets, and highly seasoned and fried foods are banned."

September 8, Meta wrote *Fudge Making Finds Favor with Co-Eds*. Meta has a lot to share with us about fudge making, especially how "It has a place in every young man's heart and every girl's category of accomplishments." Meta tells us that it is the "perfect food," as it contains both milk and sugar. Meta went to one of the few coeducational institutions in the nation in the 1910s and 1920s. This would have been unknown at many other institutions and probably frowned-upon behavior. But then Meta Given was 37 when she is writing this article and things were beginning to loosen up by the mid to late 1920s.

Upon finding the 1925 article about fudge, I also discovered something wonderful. The first picture of Meta Given which was probably taken around 1925.

September 11 there was a review of Meta Given's milk article, which looked at the positive and negative side of drinking milk. Women consider their fortune; therefore, she suggested drinking a quart of milk daily to maintain that beauty.

There is a drawback that she felt is worthy of mention, the effect on one's weight by drinking this much milk. So, the dilemma is beauty or weight. Surely, we can find a balance; even Meta would agree that compromise is imminent.

In 1926, Meta Given wrote several articles listed below:

January 1, *How Butter Fat in Milk Is Broken Up* ran in several papers including the Sundance Times. She starts out with a question challenging the reading, "Do you know what the word homogenization means?" The article educates the housewife on the difference between fresh cow's milk and evaporated milk.

When this article comes out Meta is working at the Evaporated Milk Association and still doing graduate work at the University of Chicago. The article claims Meta is a "food authority doing research work" at the university at this time.

The article has pictures to accompany the explanation which include the "Fat Globules in Raw Milk" and "Globules After Homogenization." This article is quite deep as it goes into the differences of milk and it also talks about mother's milk. "The fat in mother's milk is in homogeneous suspension and being flocculent forms small curds in the stomach," so she is describing mother's milk as being easier to assimilate by a baby.

Then she goes on to say why cow's milk is harder to digest by a baby: "the fat in the cow's milk is in relatively large globules, forms large tough curds in the stomach and is much harder to digest."

She makes a bid in this article how evaporated milk is more palatable for baby by saying *"fat is broken up by homogenization and the curds softened until ... they become a size that is possibly more digestible and "they resemble natural infant food."* The Evaporated Milk Association hired Meta Given as their first director of the home economics department to test the types of milk and their differences and uniqueness. They were very interested in getting more of their product into the hands of the American public for consumption.

Through this testing, they produced hundreds of brochures that showed all kinds of ways that their product was as good if not often superior to fresh cow's milk for a variety of reasons.

February 1's article for the *Press-Courier* in Oxnard, California was *Careful Meals Means Health for Children*. Meta Given quote from the article said, *"Modern mothers make the mistake of allowing their children to select the kind of foods they will eat ..."*

However, Meta believed that a little training by their caregiver will serve them better in the long run. The article denoted "Meta H. Given, food authority doing research work at the University of Chicago."

Food is the most important thing in health. Mothers who give their children the best possible start in life will do well to give greater consideration to diet. No child should be allowed to choose the things he will eat. Children naturally eat the foods that attract them. Often these foods are the wrong ones.

It is the mother's business to train her children to eat proper foods. She should see that her child has a healthfully balanced diet. Pure milk, whole cereals, fresh eggs, fruits and vegetables ought to have a prominent place on the child's menu.

A certain amount of concentrated food is necessary to adolescent children, for rapid growth sharpens their appetites so that they crave more food than their systems can well take care of. Many mothers have solved the problem of sterile milk by using evaporated milk, which is merely concentrated cow's milk that has been subjected to 240 degrees of heat for thirty minutes to kill all disease bacteria.

*"Wrong feeding means trouble in the stomach. It is essential that children should obtain food that is easily assimilated."*

As you can see from these articles, Meta is very authoritative in her beliefs about what children should eat and how parents should control the types of foods that children do eat. I have read in another article that children can be spoiled and allowed to refuse to eat certain foods even when company is present.

Meta, of course, finds this rude and wishes that parents would help control the situation through always making children eat what is good for them. She often gives suggestions on how to make food more appealing to children, so they will want to consume the good foods as a pleasure instead of as a chore.

February 5 article for *Press-Courier* in Oxnard, California was called *"Teach Girls to Cook, Says Expert: Ignorance of Food Ruins Health"* Teaching girls how to cook and the value of good nutrient is just as important as teaching them the "three R's." according to Miss Meta H. Given, home economist of the Better Health Bureau and a research worker at the University of Chicago. This article is the only reference that she worked for the Better Health Bureau.

"*Improper diet has ruined the health and lives of thousands of children. The blame lies with the parents. Every child ought to be taught that a well-balanced diet is absolutely essential to health and happiness.*"

"*Helping mother in the kitchen would be made a joy to little girls if mothers took the trouble to explain the mysteries of cooking and the fundamentals of nutrition to them.*"

Meta Given knew firsthand about the joys of helping in the kitchen. As we learned, Meta started cooking at a very young age and by the time she was 10 years of age she was experimenting with her own recipes.

February 2, *Scolding is Ruinous to Appetite* – I thought this article was be about scolding children, instead it is advice about not scolding your husband at breakfast time because it is ruinous for appetite and could ruin his entire day during business.

"*On the other hand, a gay word or two, a smiling face, and a well-balanced meal makes for happiness and good will.*" *She continues with the effect you can have on your husband's day that will* "*increase the working power of the man and cheer the day for his wife.*"

We can all learn from this: "*Breakfast should be served in an atmosphere of warm friendliness and love.*" While today breakfast may be served by anyone, her words of encouragement can be used today as in yesterday regardless of whose job it is to accomplish such a task,

"*It will be if the 'housewife' creates it.*" In all of her writings, you can change that word to mean anyone who prepares the meal. I believe Meta was writing for the majority of people who were doing the job of the day.

If Meta Given was alive today and writing, she would have included anyone who oversaw the task of preparing meals and all that entails.

February 9, *Emergency Pantry* – According to Meta, "*Efficiency and economy go hand in hand in the kitchen as well as in the business world.*" Meta tried very hard to show that a woman's job in the home was just as important as any business job. This was just one article that emphasized that point.

It was considered a *"new kind of pantry"* and the *"latest innovation in the cuisine of the modern housewife."* Meta also is giving the housewife with the credit of the innovation. It is a well-known fact that women have been and are the original innovators and inventors.

Meta goes on to describe the types of items that she would have in her pantry for just such an occasion when an unexpected guest is welcomed. Every woman knows that you can't have a guest in your home without offering them something to drink and eat.

She goes on to say that with these items like canned milk, meats, corn, tomatoes, and mushrooms, one *"may have two hundred or more savory dishes ready to her hand."*

The offering of something from her pantry at the ready frees her up to be *"hospitable"* to her guest instead of slaving away at *"the kitchen range."* Meta also gives other suggestions to the busy housewife like making *"a splendid luncheon or dinner in a jiffy"* especially if you wish to *"spontaneously invite a few friends for lunch at the last minute.* It can be gratifying to know that you have *"the aid of the new pantry."*

March 20, *Half of U.S. Brides Know Little About Cooking* for Huntington Herald Indiana – *"Less than half of the 1.2 million brides who set up housekeeping every year in the U.S. are competent, when they get married, to plan or prepare a meal unaided, according to Miss Meta H. Given, home economist and research worker at the University of Chicago."*

Meta Given says even though the bride of today in 1926 knew very little about meal-planning and preparing, they had a great advantage over brides of a generation ago. Those advantages include appliances, utensils and ready-made food that has low spoilage.

January 30: *The Weekly Kansas City Star*, Kansas City, Missouri advertises "Farm Women to Meet," announcing the Kansas program for farm and home week. Women heard book reviews, discussions of children's diets and other homemaking problems. Visiting speakers included Miss Meta H. Given, director of the home economics department of the Evaporated Milk Association.

1930 articles listed below:

On May 31, the *Kentucky Advocate* ran an article titled "Early Morning Plans for Meals Appeal to Brides." It contained an article to help women cut their time while cooking using an old-fashioned item called a *"fireless cooker."*

I also found this neat website describing the cooker, how to make a cooker and a whole bunch of other information. The great thing about this website is that it is designed to help people survive in the twenty-first century using nineteenth century skills. (admin, 2013)

I truly wish there was a way to teach every person the very basic skills. How to create something using the materials around them, how to cook, how to clean and everything else. From what I have read about Meta, she used all the basic skills of life.

Meta Given was an inventory of recipes. She was innovative in her style of trying different ingredients. We find that she learned much of her basics from her family. Then augmented her education through schools and universities.

A June 13 article in *The Kokomo Tribune*, from Kokomo, Indiana was Meta H. Given's *"Eggs as You Like Them are Now Plentiful."* Meta Given tells a little about eggs and how they are plentiful during the spring of the year. She also says that a famous chef (no name mentioned) says that there were more than 400 ways of serving eggs.

The two Meta mentions are frying an egg and omelets. *"With her (Nature's) own amazing magic she has combined the sunshine vitamin and an abundance of iron and phosphorous – and behold! She has created for us a most nutritious food* (unknown, 2017)."

On June 27, *The Kokomo Tribune* carried Meta H. Given's article, *"Summer Meals in a Jiffy Solve Mother's Problems."* Meta wrote about the drudgery of cooking three meals daily. She believed that she would provide in this article a quick solution to this problem between the "automatic refrigerator" and "canned" goods aplenty.

A refreshed, relaxed morning at the beach can be mother's lot during the summer. All she needs to do is *"cultivate the habit of planning meals that can be prepared in a jiffy."* Meta goes on to give us some helpful hints that can make meals in a jiffy, yet one does not have to forgo nutrition or break the budget.

October 21 *Chicago Tribune* – Meta Given writes an article about creamed soups that include sweet milk with stewed tomatoes. She was shocked when the two were combined in a class that she was attending. Why? Any farm girl would know that "such mixtures curdled" and *"naturally we concluded that a combination of milk and tomatoes could not result in a soup that would appeal to the eye and palate."*

I can see her standing there with her mouth gaping and eyes as wide as saucers. If it was not frowned upon, there may also have been gasps throughout the room. Can you imagine?

However, from the stories my great-grandmother told my mother, I would say much of that behavior would have been curtailed. When in school there were strict rules and gaping mouths, wide eyes and comments were just not allowed.

However, the women who were taking the class may very well have discussed it later. But then there may not have been any of that either. My great-grandmother when attending normal school, said that they were watched like hawks from sun-up to sundown daily. There was very little free time. If they were not in the classroom they were responsible for the cleaning and upkeep of the place as well.

In the article, Meta wrote first that she was delighted by the results. But then when tasting the soup, she realized that by adding soda, which prevented the curdling, it took the edge off the delicious tomato flavor. So, it appears the delight was short-lived by the resulting flavor tasting. Meta, of course, figured out a way to perfect the process by eliminating the use of soda and learned the best way was in the combination of the ingredients.

In the early 1930s, Meta Given mostly wrote for the *Chicago Tribune* while publishing with other newspapers. She wrote over 365 articles for the *Chicago Tribune*. During her tenure there, she was their number-one draw to the newspaper for her type of column.

Meta Given wrote the famed *"Tribune Cook Book and Food Talk"* column that was first written by Caroline Maddocks (pen name Jane Eddington) for ten years prior to Meta Given. Then it published under the name of Mary Meade after Meta Given's one-year stint. Then it was written by about five or six women, with Ruth Ellen Church writing the article until the 1970s.

Much of the experimental kitchen, photographs and other innovations can be attributed to the many women who provided their home economic skills through the years. I read in a 2015 article by Kimberly Voss that Church was responsible for the experimental kitchen and the photograph taking at the Chicago Tribune.

However, as we have learned about Meta Given who provided those skills and innovations at the Evaporated Milk Association, we can assume that she also provided them at the Chicago Tribune.

I am sure over the years there were many women who contributed to the ongoing development of the experimental kitchen, photography and such at the Chicago Tribune starting with Jane Eddington through Ruth Ellen Church. However, much documentation seems to leave out Meta Given. It may be because of her one-year stint where Ruth Ellen Church did have a 38 year history with the newspaper.

*Chicago Tribune* 1930-1931 articles by Meta Given

Meta wrote about food, but she also touched upon the importance of the role of the person feeding the family as she wrote, "There was never a job of more far-reaching influence than that of feeding the family." Meta Given believed that women were the backbone of America, that without their good judgment, their prudence, and their diligence in providing the best available food in the correct menu form that our nation would have succumbed to disease and weakness.

"*Food, without doubt, is the most important factor in our lives. It controls the destiny of individuals and nations. A child supplied an adequate diet waxes strong. One that must subsist on a poor diet grows weak. The strong resist disease and enemies, but the weak succumb to them. So it is with nations.*"

Meta wrote the service that the homemaker provides is just as important as any job in existence. She equated the task to scientific skill for an achievement that only great "*imagination, skill and individuality will accomplish.*"

"*Gathering a healthy, hungry family around the table three times a day and maintaining this vigorous condition throughout life is an achievement. It is a business with great opportunities and it pays big dividends, though imagination, skill, and individuality must be used.*"

However, we as a nation and as a world have fallen short in the skills and abilities that women used to provide for their families. But Meta Given believed that women should be proud of what they accomplish and that there is great value in what is provided by homemakers. "*Why shouldn't any woman become enthusiastic about so vital a profession? A kitchen is a woman's worktop. Its output is for health and abundant, joyful living. The scientist in his laboratory is working toward the same end. So is the artist in his studio.*"

Everyone knows that cooking is a scientific skill. It is tried-and-true combinations of ingredients that produce unique products. "*All the interesting chemical reactions and physical changes do not happen in test tubes and flasks. Just as fascinating and important ones take place in sauce pans and mixing bowls.*"

Meta Given gave credence to the skill necessary to perform the tasks, to choose the right ingredients, combine them correctly and serve them in a pleasing way to encourage the family to want to eat that which was nutritious regardless of the food.

*"The opportunity for the expression of one's artistic bent does not always come in the field of music, sculpture, and designing. The making of an attractive salad or a tender, crisp pie crust requires talent and technique; as does the painting of a beautiful picture or the rendition of a concerto. The only difference is in the effect produced."*

For instance, on June 3, 1930, Meta Given wrote about spinach. People felt an obligation to eat such food regardless of its nutritious value. She wrote, *"The tone of his voice sounded as if he had had some advice from his wife or doctor."*

She writes about the *"cause of this attitude,"* which she believed could be *"traced to poor cooking."* Meta Given believed that there were specific ways to cook just about everything. You can't just throw every vegetable into a kettle of boiling water and hope they all come out great.

Meta spent time in helping the reader understand about mineral content, which needs to be preserved and can be done so by cooking *"in an open kettle and cooked as quickly as possible to preserve the color."* Meta also suggests adding lettuce to the pot and using only the water in which you washed the for the boiling in about six to ten minutes.

In this article is her famous salmon loaf recipe, which is still a first-rate dish. I served this dish a few years ago to a delightful crowd who all commented on the dish, saying it was one of their favorites from their childhood.

So many dishes that Meta Given perfected can still be found on tables today as comfort foods. This particular-dish is only 291 calories total with 104 protein grams, 132 fat, and 55 carbohydrates.

Meta Given believed in sauces and her cookbooks are full of recipes for delightful sauces that accompany just about any dish. Her articles reference which particular sauces go with which dish, like a white or egg sauce for the salmon and French dressing for the spinach salad.

On June 4, Meta Given starts her article with "a harbinger of spring." Each season has special foods, and, in this case, she is talking about the *"first bunch of asparagus in the market window."* Meta Given teaches that each fruit and vegetable have true seasons. If we buy local, we will appreciate them best because they are *"beautifully colored and delicately flavored vegetables."*

This can be said about so many of our fruits and vegetables that are local. She tells us that *"High quality in the cooked vegetable depends on high quality of its freshness and the method of cooking."* The picture she provided in this article shows a pot cover with a center opening in which the asparagus is standing up in a boiling pot of water.

Meta recommends cutting off the tips and cook the butts first until they are almost tender (ten or fifteen minutes), then putting in the tips. In eight or ten minutes they will be tender.

So many people will not eat the butts of asparagus. I must say, this is so worth a try as asparagus is very expensive even in season. The method described dramatically decrease the overall cost of the vegetable. According, to Meta the method of cooking was invented by our grandmothers, with "inexpensive tin saucepan lids – those with concentric ridges were used.

The central circle of the tin was cut out. This lid, with the hole in the center, was placed over the saucepan of boiling water. The asparagus bunch was then inserted. When the lower part of the stalk was tender the lid was lifted off and the asparagus allowed to lie horizontally in the pan to finish cooking."

Meta Given so believed in trying to provide the correct way of cooking. You spend the time and money to purchase the product, shouldn't you get the best out of that product in aesthetics as well as flavor? And don't forget about all the nutritional value.

On June 6 of 1930, Meta Given told women that they should select food firsthand and don't leave it to a phone call to the grocer. After all, *"The modern manager of the home goes to the market and compares values in just as intelligent a manner as does her husband when he invests in stocks and bonds. She realizes that it is a 'see it yourself' job."*

She also goes on to say that a marriage is a partnership and equates it to a home business that is sure *"to prosper."* There Meta goes again equating the job the person does at home to that of an office manager in a prospering business.

Meta Given believed that anyone who works at home needs to remember that they are running a business and that they are the food manager, project manager, chef, day care provider, supervisor, trainer, mentor and so many other titles that they can equate to the challenging work that they provide in their entrepreneurship with their mate.

Meta Given shares many stories in her articles about family, and here is one that is about a friend. On June 9, 1930 in the *Chicago Tribune's "Tribune Cook Book Food Talk"* article, Meta tells a story about one of her home economic friends.

They were discussing the attractiveness of food, such as a brilliant apple or striped candy.

Meta's friend appeared to believe that *"This desire for beauty has become exaggerated."* The friend believed that color over *"desirable qualities"* of the food such as *"blue green peas"* delivered disappointment.

Meta agreed with her friend. *"I can fully appreciate my friend's rebellious feeling."* Meta's argument towards the resolution was to know your peas, after all, it is *"one of the first requisites in cooking peas."*

Meta goes on to tell us about how to consider fresh peas, and that while you are shelling you can multitask by meditation. Again, this is a green vegetable, so cooked in an uncovered vessel, with salt and the correct amount of water to vegetable 1:1 cup and a teaspoon of salt for each quart of water.

She recommends about twenty-five to thirty minutes until tender. Meta also talks about alkaline or acid water. The first is the type of water in Chicago and the latter would be created by using a cover.

An interesting twist that Meta suggested is adding a sprig of mint, which would go very well with lamb when they are served as accoutrements.

This next article written on June 10 was the first article I remember reading from the *Chicago Tribune* when doing my research. Meta starts with this opening line, *"Beautiful, golden brown, symmetrical nuggets."* Whatever she is talking about, I want some now, my mouth is watering and I can't wait for the next sentence or two that will reveal the most glorious of foods, muffins.

*"When broken apart there is revealed a delicate sponge-like texture colored like sunshine."* I can see the sun on the horizon

as she is breaking her breakfast muffin to find just how delicate it is when it is correctly made.

Meta told us that *"where she eats breakfast, they serve muffins just as she described: 'mouthwatering.'"* She finds this to be her go-to food when looking for a diversion from things like "stale toast and rolls" (Given M. , Food Talk, 1930).

Meta revealed the secret trick to making just such a mouthwatering muffin as she describes. She told us that there are many things that don't have to be just so when making muffins, like the flour. However, the assembly, timing of ingredient mixture and how much you mix the materials are key.

She wrote, *"Stir the material until the dry ingredients are only just dampened. Stop there."* This is what I love about Meta Given's recipes and discussions about the preparation of foods. She is precise (scientific), she is not condescending, but she is emphatic.

So many of her recipes and explanations could make the most successful cook/chef out of anyone. I find reading her cookbooks or articles more like a novel or a manual will lead to ultimate success. Between the cookbooks and her articles, she gives discussions about every type of food.

The next column Meta wrote was about red vegetables in the June 11 edition of the *Chicago Tribune*. In this article, she told us a personal story about her mother cooking beets, their effect on the family when placed upon the table and how emphatic her mother was about how to cook beets. I told my mother about this article and she had never heard about how best to cook beets.

Meta said it was her mother's method that she recommends, which is *"never cut into the beet, leave enough room from the stem not to puncture the beet, about four inches.*

*Wash carefully with your hands, never use a brush, as this might break off the roots."* Be very careful in the handling of the beets from cutting, washing, and handling into the kettle. Never prick the beet with a fork and so on. Meta says this is still the best way to cook this beautiful vegetable.

Meta refers to herself as a *"modern"* who needs to know the reason behind these secrets. Well, if you have ever cooked a beet and pricked it with a fork, you will soon find out the beautiful red color bleeds out in the water, leaving the beet to quickly loose its color.

This vegetable is the opposite of the green vegetable where you would cover, keeping the acid within the kettle. She claims that it takes about thirty to thirty-five minutes to cook, and you can tell if they are tender by holding one in a dishtowel and giving it a little squeeze.

Since it takes quite some time for them to cook, she recommends a steamer or pressure cooker which can cut the amount of time required for cooking. Her best suggestions for preparing are: *"buttered, pickled, salad or even a soup,"* which she claims are *"all simple ways to serve this vegetable."*

Another article I read she suggested this vegetable in the winter, as it will add much-needed color to your otherwise potentially drab-colored table.

In the 13 of June's *Chicago Tribune* column, Meta Given was talking to her butcher who shared his information of the change in the market in the last few years: *"Meat cookery has undergone a great change."* Because *"of this change, the butcher offers meat in a different form,"* is what he claimed. She tells us how the conversation started *"about the big tubful of sausage."* He said because *"it is impossible to sell certain cuts of meat."* The cuts that used to be popular were now passé because they took too long to cook.

Meta used an expression you don't hear much today: *"The cuts that used to be so much in favor for stews, post roasts or boiling go begging."* The modern woman just didn't want to take that time for cooking, after all they were getting educations, working, and they no longer could afford maids. In the past, women spent more time in the home or they had domestic help. As time went by, the maids became a luxury of the past and women's priorities shifted.

Meta offered another side of the coin that women are more willing to pay a little more to the butcher for ground meat and expensive cuts, which *"increase our gas bills in cooking and entail extra labor."* Of course, Meta Given is a scientist, so she offers the argument that through experimentation and the proper equipment you can purchase the cheaper cuts – if you use *"fireless cookers, steam pressure cookers, and ovens,"* which are used to simultaneously cook other foods.

Meta is a great advocate for the cheaper cuts of meat as they save a lot of money. One of her most popular themes is that you can have very tasty nutritious meals on a budget.

Meta Given was not a journalist like Nellie Bly, but she was an advocate for proper nutrition at an economical price. Meta did not pull any stunts or even attract attention to herself, yet she was very popular from the early 1930s through the late 1940s. She wrote thousands of articles for hundreds of newspapers throughout this nation.

In the *Chicago Tribune*'s Food Talk for July 14, Meta dabbled in talk about diets. She had heard that many women young and older were talking about diets. She listened carefully and discovered these diets were whatever the latest fads were: *"freak diets"* that might be *"tomato juice and hardboiled eggs"* or the like.

She recommended that you go to a doctor or a nutrition worker. It's interesting that she chose a doctor, because at least today, some 100 years later, most doctors know nothing about how to prescribe a proper diet to their patients. I would find it hard to believe that in the 1930s they knew this information.

However, Meta was not afraid to give her advice on this subject, as she saw it all within her realm of good health and of course nutrition. While she noted that the food she mentioned were very good and nutritious, she commented that by themselves they were *"insufficient to build a well-balanced diet."*

Leaving the woman to wind up losing her good looks and health. She believes that if a woman *"weighs not more than 10 per cent above the average for her height and age, then her weight is normal, and she shouldn't meddle with good health."* You've got to love the good, sound advice of Meta. She told it like it was, and almost demands that you listen to her good sound advice for your own health and happiness.

I couldn't help but laugh at the article published in the July nineteenth *Chicago Tribune* by Meta regarding bacon and the reason for poorly cooked bacon in Meta Given's grandmother's day: *"That bacon never curled unless it came from a pig killed in the wrong time of the moon."* She goes on to say that *"the modern cook has no such alibi."* And that *"a confession of carelessness explains poor results."*

Mint jelly and mint sauce are *"two delightful accompaniments of lamb."* There are many types of mint – thyme, spearmint, peppermint, summer savory, sage, and sweet marjoram are a few on the list. Meta continued to give us a wonderful lesson on mint's different uses from chewing gum to confections. She told us that there are two varieties of peppermint – black and white. I wonder if they grew this on their farm, as she said that black is the most popular to grow in this country.

I was reading the December 5 article in the *Chicago Daily Tribune* where Meta Given talked about getting the whole family involved in the merry-making of Christmas preparations. She painted a delightful picture where everyone is pitching in making candy, cakes, cracking nuts, decorating and even stuffing the goose.

Who are performing the tasks? The young daughter home from college might want to show off her skills she has been learning – after all, many women went to school for home economics – specifically nutrition and diet.

Then there's grandfather, who loved *"to crack the nuts"* or other tasks that if he knows how will *"make these things better than any of the younger"* generation. Meta believes by enlisting the help of all family members that *"it can be charming and spontaneous and so party-like."*

Another article that was also published in the *Chicago Tribune* on the 5th of December is titled *Green Peppers Done Thus Make A Tasty Dish, Says Meta Given*. As I read the recipe, I thought, I don't even like green peppers sautéed, however, as I was reading Meta wrote, *"calculated to make any one's mouth water."*

And sure, enough if my mouth did not water. I know it was not because of the green peppers, but because of Meta Given's suggestion. I read so many of her recipes and my mouth does water.

The recipe has you *"plunge the peppers into hot boiling fat and rub off the skins."* Can't say I have ever known anyone to do this with peppers. This may just be the perfect recipe to make peppers. But then I think that about most of her recipes.

This recipe sounded like Meta Given was quite intimate again. Another recipe published in the *Chicago Tribune* on the 5th of December. The recipe is for an Apple Sauce Spice Cake. Meta wrote, *"There is something essentially old fashioned about apple sauce spice cake. Even its name. It isn't found on many menus. It isn't served at many teas. It belongs, somehow, to the age of huge kitchens, regular baking days twice a week, the barrel of apples in the cellar, and wintry evenings around open fires."*

We know Meta Given spent her early years in a three-room homesteader's cabin in Missouri. The aforementioned description brings that picture to my mind, with her mother's homespun rug on the floor and her mother, father and sister sitting by the fire.

We can all remember a festive Christmas Eve where family and friends are getting together and last-minute preparations for the holiday brings us all together. Meta Given on December 24, 1930 tells her story of *"'Twas the night before Christmas,"* "But all through the house everyone was stirring, even the mouse." She must have read the famous "Night Before Christmas" poem. She gave her take on how merry the time was, serving light but hot refreshment with a delightful recipe of wassail.

Christmas must have been a very special time for Meta Given and her family, with family and friends all around coming and going the days before and the day of. In this article December 25, 1930, she wrote, *"The roast goose has been downed with many 'Ohs' and 'Ahs' of delight."* I believe that Meta knew all about those sounds of pleasure as the meal is being served, even as a buffet or on the table.

She talked about it often, even mentioning her father in one specific article. In this article, she warned of serving too big a meal after Christmas dinner. She claimed, *"it is unwise to further tax the stomach with a hearty supper."* Meta paints a picture: *"As darkness falls the memory of a Christmas dinner is all that is left or should be left of the bountiful feast."* You see the beautiful sunset, the table has been partially cleared away and everyone is sitting here and there, contemplating the meal, with thoughts of the next meal.

Even though Meta was writing during the heart of the Depression about a bountiful feast, there were many who would not have as bountiful feast as she and her family.

Meta was able to find work through most of the Depression, even starting her own business in 1933. With about 20 percent of the population out of work there were still about 80 percent who were not as hard hit by the downturn of the financial crisis (Depression 1929, 2017).

1938 – Advertisements and Writing Articles

Between the time Meta Given was let go from the *Chicago Tribune* and the late 1930s, she was incredibly busy. She first performed demonstrations for various venues that were very popular at the time, where home economists of various abilities gave talks and demonstrations.

Then she edited a cookbook completed for a publishing company. Through my research I found that she held the copyright for this book. I also found advertisements for a company called Fairbanks-Morse. This company was selling a new kind of refrigerator called the *"Conservador."*

This refrigerator had a door with a second door that stores your condiments. Saving the consumer time, Meta Given is the person who scientifically testing this invention and found that it saves 26 percent of your time in searching for items.

By 1933, Meta Given has started her own business: "Meta Given's Experimental Scientific Kitchens," which were up to all kinds of interesting business solutions. She lent her name and image to products. She took photos of foods that she staged for magazines and journals. She was also the *"go-to girl"* for all the major packing companies.

By the late 1930s, she was back in the business of writing articles for newspapers, giving her advice on everything imaginable relating to economy of food. The earliest paper she wrote for was on May 29, 1938 for the *Milwaukee Sentinel* out of Wisconsin in an article where she provided some of her famous recipes.

This particular one was for filled cookies. I originally got this article from the Google Newspaper Archive, it has since been taken down. You now have to go the Milwaukee Library to obtain a copy to review (Given M. , 2013).

## 1940-1949 Syndicated Columns

Starting in the late 1930s through the late 1940s, Meta Given would have one article after another splashed over the pages of newspapers from New York to California and from Washington State to Florida. She must have been a household name during this time for millions of Americans. Her fame was far-reaching through these newspaper columns.

1943 – *Harrisburg Telegraph* ran one of Meta Given's article on rationing food. Meta Given was a hometown-type farm girl who said that her family didn't have money for extras. But according to this article, her family gave her a few pennies to splurge on candy. She wrote of standing in front of a dusty candy counter contemplating her choices with the money she had to spend.

Now let's see, will it be jelly-beans? They are yummy, or how about chewy sticks wrapped in waxed paper (sounds like squirrels) for you got the most of them. But there there's jaw-breakers (these were my favorites as a kid). She equated this practice as being no different for a kid as for an adult during the war and trying to decide what to get for dinner with the precious points allotted.

I can see the sweet little carrot-top girl in her long skirt, her Sunday best, going to town, which was very seldom. Many times, it was to bring things in for sale and then exchange for the monthly supplies needed, like flour and such. Many of Meta's articles are full of such lovely memories of her childhood.

Between 1931 and about 1939, Meta spent most of her time doing demonstrations, advertising for companies like Quaker Oats and Fairbanks-Morse. The most remarkable accomplishment was the beginning of a consulting business in the middle of the Great Depression in 1933.

Most people remember Meta Given for writing two cookbooks: the *Modern Family Cook Book* and *Meta Given's Encyclopedia of Cooking*. However, Meta Given also wrote thousands of newspaper articles and columns for hundreds of papers across the nation.

I have found over ten thousand articles on the website newspapers.com. I also found hundreds more on a website called Fulton, which has well over 2,000 columns written by Meta. I believe there are thousands more of newspapers and articles to be uncovered through local newspaper and library archives.

Meta talked about food like one was having an orgasmic event. Poetry has never been as pretty as Meta's prose about food like muffins, asparagus and meringue.

Within these articles and books are bits of biographical details – as a little girl, I stood in front of the dusty candy counter. Or as a young girl, we didn't have any money. Or my father taught me the love of food. Her mother taught her how to prepare foods and was still teaching her until her mother died in 1949.

I have read that everything we write is a bit autobiographical. Meta Given proved this to be very true. Reading her work, reading bio pieces written in newspapers and piecing it all together provided the full picture of a red-headed Irish-Protestant farm girl who grew up to be one the most popular home economists who ever lived.

While I would love to continue providing you will one story after another in this chapter, I believe I may be guilty of repeating myself. No one person lives their lives without something of interesting occurring.

Meta Given's life had a few interesting events that occurred. Just one of them was that she published over fifteen thousand articles and columns in newspapers across this nation, with well over 60 million fans who couldn't wait until her next article came out tomorrow or next week.

I know I have enjoyed reading her articles, cooking her recipes and most of all writing it all down for posterity's sake in this book her biography.

# Chapter Eleven

## The Art of Cooking and Better Meals

*Dedicated to my brothers – Kelly, Reg & Will*

THIS chapter discusses the edited and revised cookbook that Meta Given did for The Geographical Publishing Co., out of Chicago, Illinois, copyrighted as The Geographic Publishing Company's 1935-1936 Edition. I have found other edition of this book as of this writing. This book was also published as early as 1932 with Meta Given associated with the book. I have also found a 1939 edition which does not mention Meta.

This book comes with twenty illustrations. They are pictures of dining in an intimate social function. It shows a lovely table setting with a tea and saucer enlarged. Then one on the other side of the first illustration is a standard modern kitchen setup of the time, around the mid to late 1930s. The next illustration shows a table setting that indicates it is correct for luncheon or supper. On page seventeen is the picture of a modern kitchen stove that should do all of the following perfectly: "broils, stews, braises, or bakes."

There are charts for beef, lamb, veal, fresh pork, and one that shows how meat shrinks during cooking. Other pictures include steak broiled just right, green stuffed peppers, baking utensils, copper cooking pans, tricks for easy cookie making, the American pie, and two that show canning tables for successful meat process and a pressure cooker, and

# MY TIME WITH META GIVEN    213

finally there is the ice refrigerator with overhead type.

The book organized differently than Meta Given's successive cookbooks. Under each category they are alphabetical, but the groupings are not.

The index includes these categories: Appetizers and relishes, beverages, soups, fish, meat, eggs, cheese and nuts, cereals, macaroni, spaghetti and rice, vegetables, croquettes and fritters, salad dressing and salads, yeast breads, muffins, and rolls; baking powder breads, muffins and biscuits; sandwiches, spreads and toasts; griddle cakes, waffles and syrups; cakes, hot desserts, icings and fillings; sauces for desserts, cookies, cold desserts, fruits cooked, uncooked and confections, pastries, custards, candy, miscellaneous, nuts and fruit candies and marshmallows, home preservation of foods, canning, canning nonacid vegetables, canning for meat, butchering time recipes, use and care of refrigerators, food value charts, diets, and carving.

Meta Given wrote in the last paragraph of her preface in the 1936-1937 book that the recipes came from three sources: the previous version of this book, an organization called The Food Departments of Home Economics, Women in Business, and are developed in her very own experimental cookery, a business called Meta Given's Scientific Kitchens.

I have reviewed the book and there is no mention of which recipes are specifically Meta Given's. The recipes are not in her future style but tend to be more in an old-fashioned style where you would provide the ingredients generally in the order in which they are to be used or added to the recipe. There is a size next to the ingredient. The recipe either is a narrative in total or the ingredients are following with instructions on preparation.

There are many recipes that I am not familiar with within these pages. Mexican chocolate compared to the normal hot chocolate recipes is coffee. There is a grape eggnog, which I must say I have never heard of or seen any other recipes. The grape eggnog has an egg, grape juice, milk and nutmeg with sugar. This is a cold drink where the egg is beaten until light, and as you add the other ingredients you beat as well. Then there is ginger punch, which has Jamaica ginger, orange juice, grated lemon and lemon juice. This one sounds pretty good, I would definitely try it.

Oatmeal soup on page thirteen is rather different. I had never heard of this soup. The oatmeal is cooked, then pressed through a sieve. Then there is a recipe for a mint julep, which I have not heard of in years. This is made with lemon, ginger ale, sugar, mint and water. Mint lemonade might be another very tasty beverage found on page twelve. It consists of sugar, mint leaves, water, and juice of lemons.

The puree of black bean on page seventeen is another product that after cooking is pressed through a sieve. She even has mock turtle soup. I have heard of this, but not seen it in a cookbook. Norwegian fish balls are made with several types of fish: perch, pike and trout; using eggs, potatoes and

# MY TIME WITH META GIVEN

milk. This recipe calls for the tomato sauce in the appetizer chapter.

There is a fine section about meats with principles of meat cookery, reasons for cooking meat, the tender cuts, roasting, broiling, pan-broiling, the less tender cuts, cooking in water (simmering) stewing, braising, soup making, economy demands use of all cuts, and ways of using all cuts of beef.

I love this section, which tells specifically what each cut can be used for and the type of cooking. The hind and fore shank is great with soups, stews and ground meat for things like loaves or patties. The round as a juicy cut can be used for steak, pot roasts, and Swiss steak.

Each cut of meat has specific things that they can be used for: chuck is good for steaks, pot roasts and stew meat when cut. Loin ends, which is sirloin, can be broiled or pan-broiled. The neck is used in mincemeat, stews and in ground meat.

She did the breakdown with beef and pork. Just to make sure you are totally economizing, she had much to say about meat sundries, which are the heart, kidney, liver, tongue, oxtail and tripe. Most people will not even think about eating these parts. But I know that liver can make for a very tasty meal as well as being very high in nutrition. It should not be overlooked.

There are many recipes that follow through on the different types of cooking, and some are creative like the casserole of beef. This recipe can use any of the cheaper cuts of beef, is braised, then dredge in flour, then added with onion, pearl tapioca, potatoes, carrots, tomato catsup, paprika and cold water. Some of the cold water is used from the pan that you used to sear the meat, or you can do this all in one pot if you use a Dutch oven that can be used on the top of the stove and in the oven.

There is a very detailed part from the U.S. Department of Agriculture Bureau of Agricultural Economics the Division of Livestock, Meats and Whole Beef Chart. There are twelve distinct cuts of meat and from that there are sections within each cut. For instance, the rib cut has four rib roasts and one short rib cuts. Or eight trimmed chuck has one and two bottom chucks roasts, three and four top chuck roasts and five to seven chuck rib roasts. This is probably why it is confusing when you are looking at cuts of meat. Without a chart like this to take to the store, the cuts of meat are a mystery.

Generally, you can go by the price of the meat as to the cut of meat. But if you are not sure, it is charts like this that can take the mystery out of purchasing meat. And the detailed information in this section of the book also takes a lot of guesswork out of how to cook the meat as well as what to serve with it to make a completely nutritious meal.

There is also a section on rabbit. Back in the day, it was very important to know how to cook this and other types of meat as you never knew what might come to the table, especially if you relied upon wild game as part of your meat sundries.

There is a section called warmed-over meats, which are a way to use leftover meats for another meal. Meta Given so loved to use leftovers, which she turned into an entirely different meal, as it was her habit to concoct her own recipes from the early age of ten.

These dishes are savory beef, ham mousse, liver patties, meat shortcake, meat and tomato pie, meat soufflé and savory hash or southern hash. The meals were all pretty quick to make, cutting your meal preparation dramatically. Once you had cooked a roast, it could then be used in another meal with a few more vegetables or other meats to make a new savory meal.

The poultry section has what to do if you kill the bird yourself or get it from market. While we are a long way away from this for most people, there are many people who are going back to raising their own poultry. Therefore, chapters like this are a blessing in disguise. This chapter is pretty detailed about dressing the bird to be ready for cooking.

There are all kinds of recipes, from fried, fricassee, steamed, with dumplings, pie, pressed or potted to smothered, pickled and even roasting. The roasting talks about turkey, but the same instructions can be used for chicken. There are also recipes for goose, guinea fowl, duck, and let us not forget about pigeons.

The next section in this book is one for sauces for fish and meats. There as some favorites and some lesser known sauces but there are many sauces: béchamel, banana, anchovy, black butter (never heard of), brown, bread, caper, celery, cheese, croquette, and tomato sauce. There are some thirty sauces in all, so you are just about covered in any kind of sauce that you could possibly want for your fish or meat dishes.

There is a small section on stuffing. Another is the classic bread stuffing, followed with the bread stuffing that has a crust. Also, bread stuffing for fish and a peanut stuffing which is recommended for chops. It sounds very good and tender the way this stuffing and the chops are cooked.

Let us not forget about the eggs. Meta Given has provided quite a few recipes for cooking the indelible egg – boiled, creamy eggs on toast, creole eggs, eggs with cheese and spaghetti, eggs with ham and tomato, French omelet, puffy omelet, and many other omelet dishes and let us not forget about the soufflé.

There is a section on cheese and nuts. Many times, we don't really know what to do with cheese and nuts. But Meta has provided some very interesting recipes which would certainly be worth a try. How about making your own cottage cheese, baked rice with cheese, cheese paste, crackers and cheese baked with milk, or scalloped toast and cheese and then there is tomato or Welsh rarebit. This is a creamy cheese sauce that can be served over toast or crackers.

For the nut section she has salted almonds, celery, nut, and potato loaf, how to shell chestnuts and bake them. There is an interesting nut loaf recipe that uses soft bread crumbs, poultry seasoning, nuts, paprika, egg, sausage fat or butter and boiling water.

Mix in the order that ingredients are given, which is the case for most of the recipes found in this book.

Then you pack all mixed ingredients into a deep well-greased baking pan and bake for half an hour at 350 degrees F. You can serve this dish with the cheese sauce.

From here we have a section on cereals, macaroni, spaghetti and rice. there is a recipe for corn meal mush, ***may polenta recipes, scrapple, noodle balls soup, noodle paste, hominy, samp (coarsely crushed white corn), Italian spaghetti, creole spaghetti, baked rice and ham, risotto, glorified and Chinese rice recipes, wheat and sausage scrapple.

The next section is cooking vegetables. Meta, as we have learned, had some very definite ideas about cooking vegetables. You would not cook green vegetables the same way you cook a red vegetable like beets. Meta said, "During heating volatile substances in the vegetable tissue are liberated, and if these substances cannot pass off with the steam, they react on the chlorophyll to produce an ugly brown color." Now you might say that is exactly what happens when some people cook their green vegetables. Another tip that Meta imparts is the saving of the drained-off vegetable water, which should be put in the soup kettle.

That kettle sits at the back of the stove for days to make the savoriest of soups. Today you could add it to a jar and keep that in the freezer until you are ready to make a soup to enhance flavor and nutritional value.

Within her recipes we find Boston baked beans, a thick puree of black beans that is put through a sieve and served with lamb, lima bean loaf, Spanish lima, cabbage cooked in milk, boiled cabbage that is attractive and flavorful, carrots sautéed and braised as well as creamed and with rice. I didn't know you could do so much with eggplant – baked, fried, julienne, or soufflé.

She also had a recipe for sautéing cucumbers – peel cucumbers, cut in halves crosswise, soak in salt water for an hour, drain, dry and dredge into salt, pepper, flour mixture and sauté in hot fat until brown and serve on toast. Definitely one to give a try.

Is there anything you can't do with potatoes? Boiled, baked, creamed, croutons, French fried, hash brown, Lyonnaise, Franconia pan-roasted, stuffed, or scalloped. This is yet another versatile food. The stuffed recipe sounds a lot like the potato skins or twice-baked potato recipes of today.

The sweet potato has some similar recipes as its white brother, but you can also glaze the sweet potatoes, which makes for a very savory dish – cut cooked potato in slices, put in a greased dripping pan, brush with melted butter or drippings, sprinkle thickly with brown sugar and bake in hot oven at 500 degrees F until glazed with melted sugar.

She also has a sweet potato custard. This sounds like it could be interesting – cooked sweet potatoes, nutmeg, eggs, brown sugar, salt and milk. Force potato through ricer, beat egg and mix with potato; add other ingredients, pour into buttered baking dish or cups and bake slow at 300-degree F until firm in center.

Preserved red cherries make a pretty garnish and a tasty accompaniment. Many of these recipes end with other foods that will go with the recipe, making it easier to figure out how to enhance the flavors and the eye appeal.

Meta Given learned this as a young girl from her mother as she stood by her elbow during many a meal that was being prepared and eventually prepared by Meta. I can image the "*Ohs*" and the "*Ahs*" when Meta Given first started learning to cook and the pride in her parents as her dishes unfolded under their very eyes.

Now I wonder why this recipe is called *Plymouth succotash*. I suppose it may have been one of the first recipes from the days of the Mayflower landing at Plymouth Rock. I did a little research and this recipe could have been used when the settlers arrived that first winter for their Thanksgiving dinner in 1621 (Tucker, 2017).

Another unusual item is salsify or oyster plant, a root vegetable in the dandelion family that tastes like oyster. There is a recipe called creamed salsify. You cut off the tops, scrape it like a carrot, cut it into quarter slices, and keep \*\*\*white in cold water and vinegar. Cook in water, drain and combine with the white sauce. This was first used around 1690-1700 by the French and the Italians.

*Samp* is dried white corn kernels that have been coarsely cracked. It is often paired with beans, like in a favorite South African recipe, and widely used across America, too.

As famous meals go – the most famous is probably the Thanksgiving meal the Indians shared with the Pilgrims. There are certain items we equate with this meal like buttered mashed potatoes or Apple pie. However, one many can agree on is succotash. Hearty combination with corn and beans. We all know that corn is as native American staple as they come.

The settlers learned much from the Wampanoag Indians such as the succotash meal which was available year-round when other foods might be scarce. It is noted that during World War II and many other economic downturns in society we look towards such economical meal combinations.

Today, nearly all succotash recipes maintain the marriage of corn and beans, but the original tough field corn and native shell beans (typically cranberry beans in New England) have largely been replaced by sweet corn and lima beans. In its many adaptations, corned beef, salt pork, potatoes, tomatoes, okra, and peppers have all made their way into the succotash pot, along with butter, fresh herbs, and sometimes even a splash of cream. A batch of succotash is a lot like a batch of baked beans, another pot-bound New England favorite.

Canning food was a great invention and I just read the other day where they unearthed some canned goods that were over 100 years old. While they didn't look that great, or hold their nutritive value, they were perfectly good to eat. This process was invented around the turn of the eighteenth century, became very popular during the late eighteenth century and continued to be a mainstay in the American fabric until this very day.

There are people out there who would never attempt canning and especially from a cookbook in the mid-twentieth century, such as the cookbooks that Meta Given wrote. I can attest to the fact that my family and I going back several generations have used these canning methods for well over 100 years with very few changes and we are all doing fine, thank you for asking.

# Chapter Twelve

## Careers

*Dedicated to my Ancestors – who would we be without them.*

WHEN I think of Meta Given and her long, illustrious career, I think of a determined woman, a hero amongst women who forged their own careers. I think of a woman who found her destiny and forged through all obstacles to master the challenges presented along the way. Meta wore so many hats – someone at a time – but most all at once. With her flaming red hair, she persevered where others dared not tread.

She started her career at the tender age of ten. This is when she started concocting her own recipes as a young budding entrepreneur on her family's Ozark farm tucked away in the hills of Missouri. Many do not think of cooking as a science, yet we know Meta was a scientist from the very beginning.

Her parents owned their own farm in the Ozark hills of Missouri. The Givens were planting crops or caring for their apple orchard. These were just some of the many chores performed. Her parents, grandparents, aunts, and uncles were the first examples for owning her own future business.

Meta tells of learning how to cook from her mother and how to love food from her father. *"Mother would stew Golden Pippin apples and bring them hot to the table in a covered tureen. Father would take off the lid; the fragrance was wonderful. Father loved them. I got my fondness for food from him* (Nickerson,

2017)." I can smell the wafting of stewed hot apples now.

Living on the farm in the Ozarks of Missouri taught Meta Given to be humble, resourceful, and creative in imagination of meal combination. Her parents were farming entrepreneurs of their day. They had a small farm, with multiple crops that needed a lot of labor in working the soil, tending the plants, trees and animals. There was also the harvest of an abundant crop that gave immediate food for meals and distribution to businesses and members of the community.

A feature that was a relatively new concept in Meta's day was the canning of products that would allow for the use of fruits, vegetables and even meat in the winter and spring when many fruits and vegetables were not available.

Canning came about during the Napoleonic Wars. The French government offered a hefty cash award of 12,000 francs in 1797 for a clever way to preserve food for long war campaigns.

In 1809, Nicolas Appert, a French confectioner and brewer, observed that food cooked inside a jar did not spoil unless the seals leaked, and developed a method of sealing food in glass jars (Nicolas Appert, 2017). The reason for lack of spoilage was unknown at the time, since it would be another 50 years before Louis Pasteur demonstrated the role of microbes in food spoilage. However, fragile and heavy glass containers presented challenges for transportation.

With the introduction of canning in the 1800s, Meta Given's family was no exception in their creative use of the new cooking invention that helped the average farm family preserve their yearly bounty.

Through the development of the canning process for both commercial and domestic, the method became very popular in farming communities all over the world. Even today, millions of people still can their bountiful harvest, if for no other reason than to taste their grandmother's goodies, which brings them back.

Meta worked hard on the farm. However, when she went from grammar school to high school, she would find a new kind of work. She would go from making her meals, harvesting crops, and canning the bounty to teaching grammar school and continuing her education in high school first, then Normal school and finally college, with a little bit of graduate work for flavor. During all this time from 1902 to 1927 she was either teaching or learning.

Meta Given moved quite easily from home life on the farm into being a grammar school teacher at the precocious age of 14 in 1902, while she was going to high school at St. James in Missouri. The teaching career lasted for over 20 years, helping to support herself through her education years.

Miss Meta Given is mentioned as the secretary representing St. James for the South Central Missouri Teachers' Association that is out of Rolla, Missouri, which is referenced on November 27 of

1909 in Missouri within the pages of *The Kansas City Star* newspaper.

"The association voted unanimously to hold the next meeting at Richland. The association adjourned this afternoon after electing these officers: ... secretary, Miss Meta Given, St. James."

The news came out of Rolla, Missouri on November 22 that the Association "will hold its annual session at Richland" as voted on at the previous meeting. "In addition to papers and addresses by prominent teachers throughout South Central Missouri, the program includes addresses by Director L. E. Young of the School of Mines, Rolla ... The meeting promises to be one of the largest held in many years."

At the same time, they hold the "inter-high-school relay race on Saturday at 4 o'clock p.m." Every high school in the association is represented by four contestants, with a loving silver cup as the prize. There is also the "annual declamatory contest which is held Saturday night and two gold medals will be awarded to the winners."

Brookfield High School had Meta Given teaching science and agriculture, making eighty dollars a month during the 1914-1915 school year. Her teaching career moved to different schools, and in 1916-1922, Meta Given taught high school in Flat River, St. François. The population of the town was 5,112 and she continues teaching home economics in the household arts as documented in the Patterson's American Education directory through multiple volumes (Patterson, 1922).

It is hard to talk about Meta's education and career separately. As we see Meta was learning and incorporating what she learned at a very early age. She continued that practice throughout her life. One was the same for Meta. She learned something new incorporate it in her daily existence, then in her teaching career, in her writings and the culmination of all her knowledge would be not one but two large volume cookbooks – *Modern Family Cook Book* and *Meta Given's Encyclopedia of Cooking*.

When you live on a farm, you start early with your education and with your first career. It was in her family's blood, as they were farmers for many generations going all the way back to Samuel Given. That same Samuel Given came to the colonies in 1738.

During her years in high school, starting in 1902, at the age of fourteen, Meta Given tells about this experience of how she lived with a Mrs. A. Mrs. A would cook up a batch of doughnuts each week, which were greedily gobbled up within a day of their making (Given M., 1930).

Meta absorbed her educational information from all sources. She would observe Mrs. A in the making of said doughnuts. Meta asked for the recipe, but as Meta learned with this recipe and others, it was more than the ingredients and the numbers they gave.

The exact measurement was just as important. For some years later, Meta attempted to make the coveted doughnut recipe only to discover something was missing or not correct in her interpretation of the recipe she had obtained from Mrs. A.

Meta Given never gave up on the idea of making the perfect doughnut recipe as she recalled Mrs. A producing and the enjoyment derived from that time in the early 1900s. It wasn't until later that she met another woman in her neighborhood who was able to help her work through the difficulties.

This is a perfect example of how Meta Given worked and reworked the recipe to perfection. Meta was not afraid to collaborate to achieve the ultimate recipe of doughnuts and so many other recipes, as displayed in her encyclopedic cookbooks.

Some of the various things Meta learned about would be the exact measurements, the quality of ingredients, and the timing of adding each ingredient. During the mid-1800s, there was a revolution in the very utensils being used and made for cooking. Mrs. A may have been using a special utensil made at the blacksmith or tin shop just for her as her measuring cup.

When that cup is compared to the standard measuring cup that is now being mass produced by a company such as Revere, that portion might be just enough of a difference to throw off the delicate balance of ingredients needed to make Meta's desired doughnuts. This revolution led to another famous cookbook author, Fannie Farmer

During Meta's high school days, she would spend time between her home away with Mrs. A and the short train ride to her home. From the St. James High School, Meta would attend the Missouri #2

Normal School founded in 1871, later called Warrensburg Teachers College and Central Missouri State Teachers College in 1919. By 1945, they had again changed the name to Central Missouri State College. And then finally the Normal school was called the University of Central Missouri in 1972.

Meta's focus was and always would be food. Food in the planting, food in the growing and caring of, food in the molecular breakdown, and food in the beneficial elements. Also, food for nutrition, diet, and delight. Therefore, she first chooses home economics education in Normal school and she continues her training in home economics in education when attending the Universities of Chicago, Missouri, and Wisconsin.

Meta started her education at the University of Chicago in 1914 and finished her bachelor's degree in education in 1924 at the age of thirty-six. Meta was working on her masters from 1924 until 1927. Making her full educational years thirty-three years in length as she was thirty-nine years old when she finally stopped going.

All the while Meta Given is starting college at the University of Chicago in 1914, the "Great War" is starting in Europe. Jane Nickerson, the Food Editor of the *Ocala Star-Banner* newspaper out of Florida during 1975 interviewed Meta Given who reflected her need of additional education in the field of home economics (Nickerson, 1975).

Meta Given's studies would cover a good range of subjects, most of them relating directly to food, some relating to textiles, a bit of sociology, a sprinkle of physical education as well as the scientific side, with chemistry in the qualitative and nutritional analysis to help with her scientific question of *why*.

Her subjects and the grades she would obtain fascinate me. She did very well in the science classes; not so well in others. She was a scientist and we need to recognize her as one. Also, we need to recognize the women who made the home economics career what it was. Unbelievable how we love to sweep these parts of our past away, like they mean nothing.

Without women like Ellen Swallow Richards, who started the whole scientific home economics movement, and Meta Given who kept it going long after Richards left us. I know we are all the richer for their work and efforts throughout the twentieth century. They taught us about nutrition, diet, the value of eating good food, and how to care for our babies and homes.

These careers are often swept under the carpet because they were deemed women's careers. They were so vital to the revolution that occurred in the world from the early 1800s through today. We so often quote our mothers and grandmothers without always understanding where that knowledge is coming from. But once the women learned to read, they had a thirst for knowledge.

The best way to get the information out was through newspapers. That is why so many women also gravitated to newspapers for the journalist careers as our food editors, local happenings, child-rearing advice as well as the "lovelorn" columns.

Many women had long careers in their newspaper columns such as Dorothy Dix (syndicated 1896-1940s), Anne Landers (syndicated fifty-six years), Meta Given (*Chicago Tribune* 1930-1931, and syndicated 1939-1949), Jane Nickerson (*New York Times* food editor 1942-1957, *Ocala Star-Banner* 1971-1973 and *Lakeland Ledger* 1973-1988), and even Mary Meade (various women, including Ruth Ellen Church for the *Chicago Tribune* 1933-1974).

Scientific women like Meta Given offered proof to the public through their educations that food was the stuff that saved lives. They obtained these educations in colleges, normal schools and high school and even through farm associations. Scientific knowledge came in the form of the latest in nutrition, diet, cooking techniques, utensils, child-rearing, fashions, exercise, and mostly good common sense about everything.

The newspaper often offered educational information like history, math and the sciences. These women did their research, provided tried-and-true recipes, menus, and patterns. While you may look back at this information and think it is antiquated, if you really look at the data, much of it is what our grandmothers and mothers quoted. They may not know exactly where they got the information, but it came to them through newspapers, magazines, journals and even cookbooks.

Useful information is what Meta Given's generation provided. Information to make us grow and prosper. Today, the headlines are full of who killed who, or the latest Ponzi scheme.

Today's information is not brand new, and the statistics are more likely to lie than to give us straight, beneficial answers encompassing the full scope of the solution to our problems.

The issue is we no longer have that network of information that is helping the general population. We have all these scientific studies, but no one is putting the information together to come up with a cohesive solution.

First it is to separate out the vitamins or beneficial ingredients. Now it is that we need the whole, like a whole apple. As in the saying of yesteryear, "an apple a day keeps the doctor away." That saying is just as relevant today as it was 100 years ago. But people believe that apples are too expensive to buy to eat on a regular basis.

Meta Given discovered during WWII that 40 percent of all potential new recruits into the armed services were malnourished. She researched and discovered this information and then made it her mission to provide data to the people who fed our young families. This information provided all of us with nutritious, as well as low-cost solutions (Walker, 1942).

She was tireless in her efforts. I look at her career and she must have worked continuously. She not only wrote two cookbooks from scratch, but she also edited, revised, and enlarged another cookbook. In addition, she continually revised both cookbooks as evidenced by the changes to many of the recipes. If you make buttermilk pancakes from the 1951 edition the recipe is not the same in the 1953 edition.

During her graduate studies at the University of Chicago she started publishing her papers in newspapers across the nation. Many of these articles ran in a syndicated fashion, showing up in various papers from 1925 through 1927.

When I wake up in the morning, I think about Meta Given's education which began very early well before the age of 10. She was so well versed in the making of food dishes she was concocting her own dishes at that tender age. Imagine your life. Think back to when you were ten. What were your noteworthy accomplishments? I know I was not concocting my own recipes, unless you can count mud pies.

Were you cooking on a regular basis? Were you so well versed in your life that you can say you invented something, that your knowledge at that time led you to be an innovator of something – anything? Not me, but that was our Meta Given.

While Meta does not share her first recipe, you can see her innovation throughout all of her "concoctions" in her life's work. Whether it was an article in a newspaper, or a description at the beginning of a chapter in one of her cookbooks, she was unique.

Meta was way ahead of her time in that she made it her life's mission to provide highly nutritious food to an entire nation at an affordable cost. This is just the very subject that plagues us to this day! Many

# MY TIME WITH META GIVEN

people do not take the time to really look at their menus on a daily or weekly basis.

Meta looked at every menu for every day and tried to provide a well-rounded complement of nutrition. Her cookbooks presented just such menus. All you should do is look at a menu for today from her cookbooks and you will find a delicious and nutritious meal at a cost that anyone can afford.

Here is a menu on page 123 from the 1942 *Modern Family Cook Book*:

*Sunday's Dinner Menu for June 23 – Stuffed lamb breast on page 531 with lamb, rice and onion; Buttered new peas on page 1060 with peas and butter; whole wheat bread and butter; raw cauliflower salad made with cauliflower, cheese, lettuce and French dressing; for dessert there is Raspberry sponge page 35 with red raspberries, sugar, egg whites, gelatin and lemon juice.* Idea: save yolks for Tuesday's menu items, and beverage always included milk for children and coffee for adults.

She covered it all with that very simple menu. She chose items that were in season for their economy. She selected a good protein in lamb. There was plenty of fiber with whole wheat bread, cauliflower, lettuce, and raspberries. These foods were economical, in season and very colorful. This was just one of 365 dinner menus.

She also provided an abundance of information about how to select food. In the choosing, she also provided where to best obtain the food. And if that was not enough, she also gave a plethora of information about the correct time of year at which to purchase the product. For instance, apples can be obtained all year round now, but at what cost? If you only buy apples when they are in season, they are cheaper, fresher and generally grown locally.

For instance, in her chapter called *"Purchasing fruits and vegetables,"* Meta Given opens with one of her famous beginnings which goes like this: *"If you've never owned an orchard, planted a garden, nor toiled in a vineyard, you'll find these pointers on quality in fresh fruits and vegetables super-profitable reading, which will help you to get your money's worth every time. Your country cousin has experience to fall back on in selecting her green groceries; you'll have this chapter* (Given M. , 1953)."

There is a lovely chart on page 239 in *The Modern Family Cook Book*, published in 1942 that is called The Housewife's buying guide for fruits, which was published by the U. S. Department of Agriculture. This chart has the name of the fruit, the unit of purchase, servings per unit, quality standards and remarks and my favorite column, season. This is so important in the actual price you will pay for a product.

For instance, apples are best purchased from the months of August through March. You may find them all year round, but if you buy them during the in-season times, they are cheaper in price. You will also find they are crisper and last longer than if you purchase them off-season.

There is also a chart on how to buy vegetables. Today we can get so many vegetables all year round. But I find things like Brussel sprouts are best from October through February. If they are purchased out of season, they can often be bitter.

These concepts were Meta Given's wheel house of information – when, what, where, how, and at what cost.

I have known many women who were directly and indirectly influenced by Meta Given and the thought process of the day. Today people say Meta's recipes are antiquated and full of unhealthy foods. But if all foods are eaten in moderation or substitutions are used, those meals take on a much healthier relevance. This is what Meta Given was all about – moderation, substitutions and an amazing cost savings.

Meta Given was the queen of economy. She, like many women who followed her advice, did what I call stretch the family dollar. In fact, Meta Given writes about it in her cookbooks. When you go to the store with ten dollars and you come out with a hundred dollars' worth of product, that is stretching your dollar.

This was another one of her documented beliefs, and she indoctrinated the American people from the late 1930s through the end of the 1940s and beyond in her cookbooks, published newspaper articles and consulting services that she provided to many companies (Kraft, General Mills, Sealtest, Quaker Oats, Meat Packers, etc.).

When did fruit and vegetables go out of fashion? Lean meat, fish and poultry: are they out of fashion?

She also has chapters on not just preparation for immediate use, but she has extensive information about the storing of the plentiful harvest. Canning and freezing warrant entire chapters on their very own. She tells us canning began in the 1800s during the Napoleonic wars.

During Meta Given's time, she and many like her perfected the canning and freezing processes. Meta Given is associated with the National School of Pressure Cooking out of Eau Claire, Wisconsin in 1932 while she is biding her time before starting her own World Class Scientific Kitchens (Given M. , 1932).

Meta Given is mentioned in several newspapers as giving demonstrations at different venues. Specific mention of her giving a demonstration for the Farm Bureau June of 1932. These processes are still being used today. Even though people today say you should "never" use the canning methods of Meta Given.

The first I heard of freezing was to blanch your vegetables in boiling water, then immediately give an ice-cold bath, then freeze – guess where they got that information? Probably a text book called *Meta Given's Modern Encyclopedia of Cooking* from 1947-1972.

Meta, we could use your sound advice today. I read over and over that to eat healthy you need to pay a lot of money (today's newspaper articles). But Meta Given's advice can still be used today. Her advice was repeated over and over again in her cookbooks, newspaper articles and journals that to eat healthy does not cost a lot, and it still holds true.

# MY TIME WITH META GIVEN

Meta Given is rolling over in her grave as I write this. She would be appalled that all of her hard work of 70 years went down the drain. Her voice of reason has no ears to hear, no voice to share and no logic to review the demanding work of yesteryear. We treat the past like it has no place in today's world.

Meta's cookbooks reeked of good sound advice. If you truly want to be healthier and live your life more economically, pick up the *Modern Family Cook Book* by Meta Given or *Meta Given's Modern Encyclopedia of Cooking*. I highly recommend we read it thoroughly and follow the great advice found within the pages of the past.

The pages are loaded with good sound advice. The recipes are so well formulated that they can withstand substitutions. Meta talked about food sensitivities, celiac and any other food substitutions needed. Yes, they were aware of many of these issues in the 1940s and 1950s.

Why didn't her books survive, you might ask? My best guess is the following. Meta had no immediate family like the *Joy of Cooking* franchise to carry on the dynasty. She had no children, and her only sibling passed away before she did. While she was an entrepreneur and she had a small staff – no one offered to carry on the legacy, like the Betty Crocker or the Better Homes and Gardens enterprises. She did not sell her scientific kitchen – she auctioned it off and sold all her items as items, not as a business.

With no way to carry on her legacy, it died out with her. More is the pity.

Going back in her career, starting in 1925, Meta Given would switch careers from home economics teacher to home economics advisor for various organizations until she became the director at the Evaporated Milk Association. In the Chemical Bulletin's February 1925 publication, The Evaporated Milk Association introduced new members, one of them being Meta H. Given.

She was the first director of the home economics department for over five years. This organization was created by the evaporated milk manufacturers to help market their products. She was responsible to "conduct research and educational work for education of the public as to character, quality, convenience, economy and general virtue of evaporated milk."

In the article, they gave a little bio piece saying, "She was graduated from Warrensburg, Mo. State Teachers College and the University of Chicago. She is a member of the American Home Economics Association (Introducing New Members, 1925)."

During her tenure at the Evaporated Milk Association, she would write many articles and papers. Many she did not get specific credit for, with the exception of one that was published by the American Chemical Association Vol20. No9 9/1928. This paper was a scientific paper on "Texture of Ice Creams." Very interesting how she used different types of milk products to make ice cream – talk about a yummy experiment.

She wrote thousands of articles for newspapers across this nation, becoming a syndicated columnist writing alongside people like Dorothy Dix, who they claim reached an audience of 60 million people in her heyday, which happened to be Meta's wheelhouse as well (2017).

And if that is not enough, how about all of the photographs of food that she took from about 1933 until 1949, when she closed up her scientific kitchen? She is not credited with any of the photographs that her company produced. She mentions the line of business when she talked with Jane Nickerson in 1975 interview for the *Ocala Star-Banner* newspaper out of Florida.

She had her very own scientific kitchen called Meta Given's Scientific Kitchens, making her one of the best-known entrepreneurs in the 1930s through the end of the 1940s. Only, she and no one else referenced her business as an entrepreneurship. She said she just hung her shingle out. That was Meta Given, humble to the core.

Within the walls of her scientific kitchens, she provided training as advertised in the newspaper. She also provided demonstrations and training at fairs, and even at Gimbel's department stores throughout her lifetime. Her early career of teaching paid off as she would teach most of her life, first grammar school, high school, junior college and then adults.

She was very popular; every newspaper that ran her column was very proud of her and her accomplishments. Today through newspapers.com you can read many glowing articles about Meta Given as the home economist, nutritionist, dietitian, author, journalist, photographer, and canning expert to name just a few of her many careers and accomplishments.

Getting back to Meta's education, which was a degree in education. This may be true, but there were a lot of home economic courses within her studies: many subjects that include but are not limited to home economics of problems in experimental cooking, elementary sewing, elementary agriculture, scientific basics of management, school of botany, elements of gardening, elements of organic food chemistry, theory of teaching food and home management, textiles, the study of sociology, organic chemistry, chemistry of food, methods of teaching, technique of instruction in high schools, experimental cooking, chemistry of food, dietaries, chemistry qualitative analysis, physical ed, medical inspection, industrial education, chemistry of nutrition, and many other subjects as documented within her transcript from the University of Chicago.

The 1930 U.S. Census has Meta Given as a Dietitian for the Milk Industry. As noted in her transcript from the University of Chicago, she had incomplete work in the Winter Semester of 1927 at 39 years old. Before July of 1930, Meta was let go from the Evaporated Milk company, the cited reason was the economy. The "Great Depression" occurred in 1929 which dramatically changes many people's lives.

By July of 1930, she obtained the job as Food Editor for the *Chicago Tribune* after ending her association with the Milk Industry. We find her working very hard for the *Chicago Tribune* writing over 365 articles in just one year; that is about one article per day.

This career was just the beginning of her prolific article-writing for the newspaper industry. She was such a big hit that she was the primary reason that readers of the women's section obtained the *Chicago Tribune*.

This was noted in a survey the newspaper did of its readers published on July 30, 1931 in *The New York Sun*. Of the 1,020 readers surveyed, Meta Given's articles were read by 919: that is 90.36 percent of readers and only 98 or 9.64 percent said they did not read her articles.

At the time, the *Chicago Tribune* boasted it was the World's Greatest Newspaper and that more than 805,000 papers were sold daily, with a whopping 1,075,000 papers sold on Sunday. The *Chicago Tribune* also boasted that "the *Tribune* is able to produce results on more advertising addressed to women than is carried by any other Chicago newspaper."

However, while it seems that she was in the middle of a great career, the *Chicago Tribune* let her go, citing the downturn of the economy again – "The Great Depression" – as the reason for her termination. Meta Given was forty-three years old in 1931. Personally, I think there was a little something suspicious about them letting go their top draw at a nationally famous newspaper.

I contacted the *Chicago Tribune* on three separate occasions for information about her employment with them. They said they had no record that Meta Given ever worked there. However, Meta mentioned it several times. I found over 365 articles either about or written by Meta Given, and they even placed an ad claiming she was their number-one draw and what a great newspaper they were for having such great staff writers. Hmmmmmm!

After leaving the *Chicago Tribune*'s employ, Meta Given started her own business as a home economist opening a scientific kitchen that she acquired in Chicago found at 155 East Superior Street. During this time, she hired a small staff of about four people who help her with her consulting jobs.

This business provided consulting assistance for many of the major packing companies (1943) as well as her writing assignments of articles. She edited a cookbook called the *Art of Modern Cooking and Better Meals* in 1935-36.

She also worked in a new field, photographing food that she prepared for use in magazines, newspapers, journals and pamphlets. Meta Given notes that photographing of foods was in its infancy at the time in an article that Jane Nickerson wrote about her in 1975. Meta Given never got any credit for her photographs. Getting credit for photographs wasn't always done in the day for Meta Given and her organization. This was a sideline for Meta Given.

The Meat Board Report of 1932 on page 15 of Volumes 10-62 document that Meta Given was associated with the cookbook *The Art of Modern*

*Cooking and Better Meals: Recipes for every occasion.* The *New York Evening Post* of January 12, 1932 mentioned Meta Given of the National School of Pressure Cookery in Eau Claire, Wisconsin as a demonstrator to Address Farmer's Week Groups in East Lansing, Michigan.

*The Ames Daily Tribune* of Iowa and the *Muscatine Journal and News Tribune* mention Meta Given Chicago Teacher and Writer on home economics subjects to give a meat canning demonstration in their January 27, 1932 edition.

The June 10, 1932 edition of the *Daily Herald*, a Chicago newspaper, said that "at 2 PM daylight savings, Meta Given of the National School of Pressure Cooking of Eau Claire, Wisconsin, will give a demonstration on the canning of fruits and vegetables at the Community house at Glen Ellyn."

This article notes that Miss Given was formerly head of the home economics Department of the Evaporated Milk Association of Chicago, and the home economics editor of the *Chicago Tribune* for one year. "This canning demonstration is scheduled as part of a regular Food Program for next year but will be held this month so that the principles can be applied in this years' canning. Everyone is invited to attend."

Canning is one of those things that you need to know when the fruit and vegetables are ready, so the timeliness of the demonstration was very important at the time of year that it was to be given. While you can learn about canning any time, it is best to know the information when you need to utilize timely canning skills.

In 1933, the City of Chicago hosted the World's Fair that was called "A Century of Progress International Exposition" featuring every color of the rainbow. The only mention of Meta Given's association with the fair was an advertisement she placed in the *Jefferson City Post-Tribune* and the *Daily Capital News* to rent rooms to fairgoers who might be in town and needed a place to stay.

With over 48 million guests to the fair within a two-year period of time, Meta Given did her part by providing three rooms to rent with "Double garage free to those driving car. Other transportation to Fair by Rapid Rock Island Express or trolley. Own car can be driven all the way to grounds along boulevards. Substantial and good breakfast provided, if desired. Room and breakfast $1.50 a day per person. Room $1.15."

Meta Given lived in her Chicago home with her mother through most of her career once she became a home economist. Meta lived in a home that was lined with trees along the boulevard. The home no longer stands. I found another address in Chicago were Meta used to live an apartment building that no longer stands.

Meta Given was far-reaching in her heyday. You can find mention of her all over specific sites on the Internet, like newspapers.com, news.google.com/newspapers. When I first started researching information about her, there was almost nothing. But as I started digging and the years went by, the information began to trickle in. There would be a book here, an article there and then all kinds of references from her career, her education right down to very personal details.

In a book written by Anna Bernedetta Towse and William Scott Gray on page 2 of their *Health Stories Book Three* published in 1935, the authors write "For valuable critical help on Health Stories Book Three gratefully acknowledgement is made to ... Meta Given, Home Economics Consultant..."

There were several references to the cookbook *The Art of Modern Cooking and Better Meals: Recipes for Every Occasion* which was published in 1936-1937 by the Geographical Publishing Company out of Chicago, IL. This book sold during 1936 and 1937, however, there are references to Meta Given being associated with this book as early as 1932 in the Meat Board Report.

During Meta Given's lifetime, she became involved with the apprenticeship of young girls through the American Home Economics Association. Meta and her associates from the Chicago section of the Home Economics Women in Business were very active in this organization. Members of the committee were Dean Mary Matthews of Purdue University, in Lafayette, Indiana and famed Dr. Evelyn G. Halliday of the University of Chicago.

This kind of assistance for young women who were completing various degrees relating to home economics made it a lot easier to find careers in their chosen fields.

Apprenticeship in Benjamin Franklin's day meant that you had to work for many years doing the bidding of your "employer." Benjamin Franklin was bound to his older brother James for nine years. Upon his last year he was to be paid journeymen's wage. Benjamin did not last the full nine years; he ran away to Pennsylvania (2017).

Many people today work as apprentices, or we call them internships or externships. Generally, the timeframe is much shorter than years, such as three months or two years.

Most people are paid, however, if you want to learn badly enough then some will do it for free, and many often get hired after their apprentice program is complete.

Truly, it is a wonderful way to get your foot in the door of a profession and business that you might not otherwise have gotten an opportunity to have accomplished without the apprenticeship (Apprenticeship in history, 2017).

The apprenticeship option has been around for a long time. It is a great way to get your foot in the door. Leave it to Meta to mentor the next generation.

We have learned so much about Meta Given from newspaper articles. For instance, the building in which Meta Given had her experimental kitchen in Chicago is still standing. She purchased the kitchen in 1933 and had the kitchen until 1948. Meta had a very long career, but her best years were from 1931 until 1948 when she ran her own business as an entrepreneur.

Meta Given's Experimental Kitchens - On November 25, 1937 there is an advertisement in the *Oak Park Oak Leaves* newspaper on page 32 for Meta Given's Experimental Kitchens located in Chicago, Illinois. The advertisement is for Cooking Classes by Meta Given. My sister and I mused at how great it would have been to have actually taken a cooking class from the master herself.

Meta kept her staff busy editing a cookbook, providing consulting services to packing companies and photographing food. This information was so generously provided by Jane Nickerson who interviewed Meta in 1975. Meta admitted that there was not always enough work to keep her staff busy which led to her first cookbook.

The first book was published in 1942 called *The Modern Family Cook Book*. This cookbook is nationally popular as a family cookbook and a text book sold to the home economics departments of Carnegie Institute of Technology, the University of Chicago, University of Oklahoma and many other great educational institutions as documented in The Wisconsin State Journal for an advertisement article promoting Meta Given's feature article called *How a Family of Four Can Eat Well on $14 per week*.

I have found the *Modern Family Cook Book* to be in over 250 institutions worldwide including Australia, Spain, the United States, and England.

Is it a cookbook, is it a novel, is it a textbook or is it a research resource? It is all of these things. Meta Hortense Given created the cookbook of the century. She revolutionized the cookbook industry. With hundreds of cookbooks on the market Meta Given's stood out among all the rest. With cookbooks like Fannie Farmer's, Betty Crocker's, The *Joy of Cooking* and *Better Homes and Gardens*, Meta Given's cookbook is a sure bet to give each of these great cookbooks a run for their money.

1942-04-09 *Pittsburgh Post-Gazette* Meta Given to lecture on Cookery bio piece says "Miss Given is nationally famous as a home economist. She is the author of one of the most complete up-to-the-minute cook books, *The Modern Family Cook Book.*"

1943-02-05 *Wisconsin State Journal* does a Bio on the "Distinguish Food Authority and Noted Food Expert." They write, "Miss Given has for years been the food consultant for America's largest packers and has created recipes used today in every American home."

That is quite the statement that she has created recipes used in "every" American home. I do know that by 1943 Meta Given was providing recipes in newspapers in every corner of America and every city and town in between. She very well could have been read by over 60 million readers nationwide.

As a graduate of the University of Chicago, the administrator of their home ec. and household department says, "Meta Given is one of our outstanding graduates."

Meta's intimate knowledge leads to her ability to advise in all the problems facing the modern caregiver. These words could have been written today as well as then. I often find myself checking her words of wisdom time and again.

"Differing from all other food services, Miss Given emphasizes the practical and usable in foods and will prove a real aid to the busy housewife who has neither the time, money nor ration "points" to devote to fancy and costly dishes. It is based on two fundamental points, cost and nutrition, both so important in war-time economy. Her food budget of $14 is designed to fit the pocketbook of the average American home and is based on the advertised sale prices of foodstuffs in Madison local stores. The nutritional content at all times meets or betters the U.S. government's 'Nutritional Yardstick' of the kind and quantity of food essential for good health. Today as never before, nutrition and health are synonymous."

In 1944, the Waterloo Daily Courier took out a full-page ad that Meta Given would be writing the *"Food Budget Planning"* article, touting that she has worked for the *Chicago Tribune* as a food editor for ten years, when in fact she worked for them for one year. However, she had been working for ten years lecturing throughout the country and consulting for many of the country's leading food industries like Kraft, General Mills, and Sealtest.

Meta Given's next big project was called the *Meta Given's Encyclopedia of Cooking* cookbook. It is the masterpiece of Meta Hortense Given. She started writing the book more than two years prior to its publication, which debuted in 1947 with a mere 16,000 copies in its first printing.

However, she sold close to two million copies by its final printing in 1972. This tome required the assistance of twenty-five people, which included her staff, friends and associates who assist in one capacity or another over that time period.

Meta Given published the *Encyclopedia* or *Bible* as some refer to it in 1947, and she was fifty-nine years young. While many people would be winding down their careers, Meta Hortense Given seems to be just getting warmed up with her second cookbook.

In 1949, Cecily Brownstone, the Associated Press (AP) food editor, wrote an article called "The Cook Goes into Library" featuring Meta Given's *Modern Encyclopedia of Cooking* in two volumes, published by J. G. Ferguson and Associates, Chicago.

"Miss Given has had years of experience in the food field, including the running of her own well-known experimental kitchen. Her recipes show careful testing, good judgment in selection, clear and thoughtful terminology. There's a wealth of supplementary cooking information along with them. This cookbook should be a great help to the novice or experienced cooks." This article ends with Meta Given's gingerbread recipe.

The following comes from the jacket of *Meta Given's Encyclopedia of Cooking*, which gives a great description of Meta's book and her way of thinking about what the average American cook and home economist student needed in a reference manual: "The most helpful, most practical cook book ever published."

While there is always a lot of propaganda when marketing a book, I know this cookbook with its 1,700 pages was and still is one of the most helpful cookbooks ever written and published. The cookbook was written in such a way as to be a clever guide for the novice or the expert.

Meta was hoping to entice every person who had to cook to find their way to be the most successful "chef" they could be for their family, friends, and important guests at any given time. Based on the menus provided, they were for everyday and special occasions.

Meta honestly believed that with her cookbooks as your second pair of hands to guide your every nuance in the cooking arena, you would gladly do the cooking with a light skip in your walk as you went through the everyday chores needed to complete the meal process, from planning to cleanup.

With such honest and simple recipes, and menu preparation at your fingertips, the shopping list wrote itself. The nutritional economical diet necessary to entice your family would leave your family breathless from the many choices that would be talked about for ages to come.

I cannot tell you how many times we enjoyed successful meals prepared by my mother and aunt, both experts at hundreds of successful meals at their humble tables. Never a complaint or a nose turned up because something was ill prepared.

Mealtime was a favorite in our family where everyone enjoyed lively conversations over sumptuous meals that were fit for the king and queen who we were surely ready should they have graced our table unexpectedly.

In the acknowledgement section of Meta's book, Meta gives this information about Elvera Rest: *"who came from the staff of the department of home economics at the University of Illinois became my chief cook book builder assistant. For more than sixteen months she applied herself capably and unstintingly to the serious business of revising old material, helping to write the new, editing and putting the copy together in logical order."*

Elvera Rest wrote the forward of Meta Given's *Encyclopedia of Cooking* cookbook. Elvera N. Rest was born February 17, 1918 in Illinois and died in Mission Viejo, Orange County, California on September 12, 2004.

Elvera Rest said the following about Meta Given: "The wise and friendly council of Meta Given." "Meta Given began cooking as a small girl on a Missouri hill farm where folk had good but little variety. The women were forced to be resourceful in presenting the same simple foods in a variety of interesting ways ... she acquired from her parents a deep appreciation for the goodness of earth's bounty. "

Elvera emphasizes the importance of a "complete" cookbook throughout her foreword that she wrote in Meta Given's Cookbooks. Elvera equates this cookbook as a second pair of hands in the kitchen: "personal shopper, a friendly dietitian" and like a "dictionary and an encyclopedia are to a writer." Elvera gives a: "For instance, perhaps company drops in on Sunday night and every store is closed."

# MY TIME WITH META GIVEN

What would someone do if they did not have the knowledge provided by this cookbook to have what Meta Given has often referenced as the "Emergency Pantry?" She also points out a tale about a teenage daughter wanting to learn to bake, turning to the chapter and verse of the item she desires and is just waiting within the many chapters of Meta Given's Encyclopedia. Elvera adds that this cookbook can improve the quality of your cooking, or provide you with specialty information on certain foods, this one book has all your basic and complicated needs in the kitchen.

Elvera goes on to say, "You'll want every recipe to produce an eye-appealing, appetite-stimulating product, as well as to include newest approved techniques, labor-saving methods, and suggestions for money and time-economy in cooking." This is the book that provides not only eloquence, but economy while you are the star of your family, friends and associates.

In addition, Elvera tells about "producing recipes that meet this standard is very serious business." Meta Given had a very modern scientific kitchen with people trained in home economics, which covered all the subjects in this *Encyclopedia*.

Elvera points out that if you follow the instructions given in this manual that you can accomplish the exact same results that were produced in the test kitchen that was used to produce this work of art.

Elvera tells about how laborious it was to write this all-encompassing cookbook and how the author had what she "called a 'feeling' for food ..." Elvera goes on to say that "a keen interest that may have started merely with an appreciation of delicious food, well prepared. It calls for study in many fields, home economics, dietetics, nutrition, chemistry, bacteriology, physiology, art, and economics, to name but a few."

Elvera goes on to say, "But the end of formal education is only the beginning for a cookbook author-to-be." While it may take years to perfect what Meta accomplished, Meta could cut the amount of time it would take you to learn to do all the tasks needed to be a successful cook, chef, dietitian or even a nutritionist, just by reading her cookbooks.

While it would be great to provide exactly what Elvera and Meta said directly from her cookbooks, it is not possible to do so, as generally you can quote a book, but to quote page after page might infringe upon the rights of the original writer.

Believe I have tried to do justice to Meta by providing a few quotes but have written the story as fully as it can be written now that just about everyone who ever worked with, taught and learned directly from Meta would have passed away. Even Meta has passed away, as long ago as 1981. As I write this that was thirty-seven years ago; while not a lifetime, certainly long enough ago that everyone would be gone or scattered in the winds.

As if this were not enough, Meta was not just writing cookbooks during the 1940s she was also writing newspaper articles and pamphlets from as early as 1939 through 1949.

Meta Given's business the scientific kitchen provided consulting to packing companies, articles to various newspapers, builders of cookbooks and she also provides cooking classes either at her place of business or at department stores such as Gimbels and at universities or fairs.

Meta Given's business continued to thrive for more than 18 years, bringing us to 1948 when she may have had her heart attack. Near the same time, Meta lost her mother and mentor soon after her mother's birthday on April 11, 1949.

Around this time when Meta had her heart attack and lost her mother she was advised to take it easy; she was over sixty years of age. Meta Given closed up her business of over eighteen years and moved to Florida.

Retirement for some would be the end of working, however, she continued to publish her cookbooks and concoct new recipes. She would continue to edit her books until 1972.

After selling approximately four million copies of her books to the public and many prestigious universities, her cookbooks were no longer published. She had a pretty good run of it, from 1942 until 1972 with thirty years in print.

Meta Given started working at the age of fourteen years old in 1902 and didn't stop completely until she was in her eighties in 1972. Even after that she could be found at her kitchen table continuing to cook until she passed away in 1981 at the age of ninety-three.

She was tall at the height of 5'8" and wore her hair in a braid that wound around her head like a crown. She was interviewed by Jane Nickerson in 1975 for an article that ran in the *Ocala Star-Banner* and *Lakeland Ledger* newspapers. Part of that article was republished as a tribute to Meta Given after she passed away in 1981.

Meta did not know why Jane Nickerson wanted to do an article about her. But for Meta Given's many fans, we are glad that Jane did interview Meta, as it gave us some personal information that we cannot find otherwise at this time.

Meta Given wore many hats during her lifetime - daughter, sister, recipe inventor, teacher, and secretary of a school association, as well as a student, author, editor, consultant, home economist, dietitian, scientist, demonstrator, mentor, judge, nutritionist, photographer and so many more.

Meta Given was a tireless learner and trainer. She believed that there was always another way to cook and combine so many foods. As we see in her cookbooks and articles, she never stopped trying to reinvent the apple pie.

Today we would probably find her taking her recipes and making them available to people with food sensitivities, allergies and for celiac disease. She had even mentioned in her cookbooks that she knew about the wheat sensitivity that people may have. As it was in the day, there was very little mention of celiac disease or food sensitivities in general.

# MY TIME WITH META GIVEN

Meta Hortense Given worked endlessly in her pursuit of providing new information to the public about food, diets, menus, calories and how to best prepare those foods. She also provided families with nutritious food without breaking the bank. She was able to provide the average housewife with the tools to make the best meals for her family at any economic level.

Meta knew and understood that nutritious food was paramount for the family and she wrote thousands of articles, pamphlets and books hammering home the "how-to's" to accomplishing nutrition on a budget. She made it seem like the easiest task to accomplish.

She often said or indicated that information was like a second pair of hands in the kitchen and at the supermarket in the choosing of the right raw ingredients to make the most delightful of meals that were not only delicious but also beautiful to behold.

Many people today find her methods antiquated. However, I believe if you substitute the words housewife and homemaker you might find her verbiage less antiquated. She used the verbiage of the day. She was certainly not trying to put anyone down or make the job of the homemaker any less than it was. She realized that it was mostly women who were providing the skills of cooking, grocery shopping, canning, etc. that households utilized in the day.

In one of her articles she equated the work of the homemaker to that of the business man. The homemaker would have to know the family budget much as a business man would need to know his budget. The homemaker needed to be a planner, a project manager, a skilled mathematician, a scientist in regard to food nutrition, and a medical doctor in the care of her family. Today we run to the doctor all the time. Back then, Mom was the family physician taking care of most of the ills for the family and neighbors.

She also realized that not all women stayed at home providing these services. She knew that many of them worked. There might also be the challenge of a single dad. While I so often hear people say that it was uncommon for women to work around the turn of the twentieth century, that is actually not true. Many women worked, and probably many more would have worked if there weren't so many obstacles in their way.

One of the few careers that was dominated by women and we seldom see women being let go in is this field known as home economics. Men were not interested in pursuing this "woman's" career, so there was very little fear associated with being "let go" for women.

1950-02-01 – Mary Mead of the *Chicago Tribune* does a short bio of Meta Given "Two of the "writingest" food experts in business were Leonore Dunnigan Freeman and Meta Given. Meta Given was one of the first home economist to set up one of the first freelance experimental kitchen in Chicago in 1933 ..."

Some people believe that it was impossible for women to have their own businesses, to be scientists or even write important books. But we find Meta Given doing all of this and so much more. While doing her business she had important "... clients ... food manufacturers, distributors and advertisers." She worked on "recipe development, booklet preparation and food photography" among so many other consulting services. Many of her services are not specifically documented except in newspaper bio pieces that were written for the "women's pages."

I have found no personal papers, no family, no colleagues nor businesses that can corroborate her work. However, there are thousands of newspaper articles that speak volumes. The books she wrote with the kind words of Mary Meade, Elvera Rest and all the nameless women who wrote on her behalf.

Meta's father's parents had been farmers since at least the 1570s in Scotland. Each family passed down their vast knowledge from one generation to another until it culminated in one Meta Hortense Given. She would do them all proud. She would take the careful lessons from her mother and her father and turn them into a writing, demonstration, photographic essay and various other consulting career skills as an early entrepreneur in the mid-1930s.

Is there a summary to Meta Given's life? I found each little bit of her life one newspaper page at a time. She came alive through her writings and her teachings which included three cookbooks. Meta was not the first and she will never be the last. But I hope you agree with me that her accomplishments were very important. That importance carried us into the 21st century with her living legacies -- books and newspaper articles.

"If there's a book that you want to read, but it hasn't been written yet, then you must write it." (Toni Morrison) This is what Meta Given and I have done!

# Timeline

| | | |
|---|---|---|
| Birth | 1888 | Date of Birth: January 25, 1888 Place of Birth: Bourbois, Gasconade County, Missouri, USA |
| Age 02 | 1890 | Carrie Given is born, sister to Meta |
| Age 09 | 1897 | Meta cooks lunch for father and farm hands – mom is away at sick neighbor – meal: turkey, cake – first recollection of cooking solo. |
| Age 10 | 1898 | Cooking and concocting her own recipes from plentiful food stuffs from her family farm. |
| Age 12 | 1900 | U.S. Census Mettie (Meta Given) James Henry (Father) Elisa Ann (Mother) and Carrie (Sister) |
| Age 14 | 1902 | Teaching Grammar school children at Oak Forrest School in the County of Gasconade and she starts high school in St. James, Missouri |
| Age 14 | 1902 | Mrs. A. teaches Meta to make doughnuts and shares recipe while Meta Given is boarding when away from home to attend school |
| Age 21 | 1909 | Meta Given is elected as the Secretary of the South Central Missouri Teachers Association in Rolla, MO. She is representing St. James School district – Meta has been teaching for seven years. |
| Age 22 | 1910 | Teaching High School Chemistry, Science and Agriculture |
| Age 22 | 1910 | U.S. Census – Meto (Meta) Given, James Henry (Father), Ann (Mother) and Carrie (Sister) |
| Age 26 | 1914 | Matriculates at the University of Chicago |
| Age 28 | 1916 | Meta Given Teacher at Flat River Junior College, St. Francios Co., Pop. 5112 teaching Household Arts in Missouri - Meta taught for many years as docmented in a bio piece in the Gasconade Newspaper in April 18, 1940 |
| Age 29 | 1917 | Meta continues teaching Junior College Courses while attending College until 1922 |
| Age 32 | 1920 | At the Universities of Chicago, Missouri and Wisconsin |
| Age 32 | 1920 | U.S. Census James Given (Father) and Ann Given (Mother) (Meta and Carrie have moved out at this time with no record in census data – Meta may have been living at the University of Chicago or some other rental housing situation |
| Age 32 | 1920 | Meta's father dies in March, James Henry Given father |

| | | |
|---|---|---|
| | | and husband to the Given women, who is buried at Union Cemetery in Bland, Gasconade County, Missouri, USA |
| Age 35 | 1923 | Evaporated Milk Association is formed by the manufacturers – "to institute and conduct fundamental research in the public interest and to develop an educational program to apply the fundamental information obtained by research." |
| Age 36 | 1924 | She graduates on June 20 from the University of Chicago - 10 years after her matriculation |
| Age 36 | 1924 | Writing articles for papers, those articles get picked up by newspapers throughout the country. |
| Age 36 | 1925 | Starts Graduate School at the University of Chicago January 02, 1925 |
| Age 37 | 1925 | Early in 1925 Meta Given joins the Evaporated Milk Association as the first Director of the *Home Economics* Department |
| Age 38 | 1926 | Writing articles about fudge, milk, brides and the emergency pantry in articles picked up by newspapers all over the nation. |
| Age 39 | 1927 | Meta continues with her graduate program - she does not obtain her masters at the University of Chicago because of career pursuits as a home economist for the Milk Association |
| Age 37-42 | 1925-30 | 1930 census data confirms working in the Milk Industry as a Dietitian this is confirmed through various newspaper articles, the jacket on her cookbooks and an article written by Jane Nickerson of the *Lakeland Ledger Newspaper* in 1975 |
| Age 42 | 1930 | Establishment of the Experimental Kitchen – "A fully equipped experimental kitchen was established in 1930...first maintained by the industry...home economics staff developed recipes...services expanded to...food photographs with accompanying recipes..." Quote from E.H. Parfitt of the EMA, Development of Evaporated Milk in the United States |
| Age 42-43 | 1930-31 | Working for the *Chicago Tribune* as Food Editor/Journalist - she writes over 365 articles in the year she spends at the *Chicago Tribune* – column called *Tribune Cookbook* and *Food Talk* – she would be the only Editor to use her own name in writing this column that was written by about 7 people using pseudonyms. |
| Age 43 | 1931 | Survey taken during her time as the Food Editor for the *Chicago Tribune* saying that the readers are most interested in her work/articles of all articles on the "Woman's" Pages of the *Chicago Tribune* |
| Age 44 | 1932 | Writes for the *Schenectady Gazette*, October 30, 1931 – "Quality in Peas is not founded alone in Price." This article is quite lengthy and has several subheadings: |

# MY TIME WITH META GIVEN

| | | |
|---|---|---|
| Age 44 | 1932 | Slower in Growth, of Different Sizes, and advice on Buying – Meta's best advice: "that will depend." The *Daily Herald* out of Chicago, IL on June 10, 1932 has Meta Given associated with the National School of Pressure Cooking of Eau Claire, Wisconsin who is providing Canning Demonstration for the Home Bureau. Miss Given was formerly head of the Economics department of the Evaporated Milk association of Chicago and was home economics editor of the *Chicago Tribune* for one year. |
| Age 44 | 1932 | November 29, 1932 the *Freeport Journal-Standard* out of Illinois advertise the programs to be presented by the Ogle Farm Group – Schedule for Annual County Institute Sessions to be held in two-day groups in December at Forreston, Polo, Lindenwood with Miss Meta Given providing the canning demonstration. |
| Age 44-85 | 1932-72 | Meta starts her own business – see break down of her accomplishments below |
| Age 45 | 1933 | Meta Given starts her own business by purchasing a scientific kitchen she calls Meta Given's Scientific Kitchens in Chicago, Illinois. |
| Age 45 | 1933 | The World's fair of 1933 – A Century of Progress – Meta was busy starting her business, but was she too busy for a visit or two to the fair? She did provide accommodations to the weary traveler at her home, which came with a garage. |
| Age 44-51 | 1932-1939 | The Art of Modern Cooking – Published with Meta Given as Editor and expanding the publication around 1936 |
| Age 52 | Circa 1940 | Through her association with the National Canning company, Meta writes several pamphlets/books about canning. "Safe Home Canning" by Meta Given, home economics Specialist, circa date of 1940s. Alibris ID: 10597847154, published by International Harvester Co., Chicago, Il She performs many demonstrations and lectures on canning from meat, fruit, vegetables, etc. |
| Age 54 | 1942 | Publishes her first cookbook *The Modern Family Cook Book* on February 2, 1942 U.S. copyright granted |
| Age 59 | 1947 | Publishes her second Cook Book *Meta Given's Encyclopedia of Cooking* which is a two-volume reference manual published for the public as well as many universities including University of Chicago, Missouri, and Wisconsin |
| Age 44-60 | 1931-48 | Meta Given has a small staff that she keeps busy with many consulting jobs that include preparing food for photographs (a new industry), scientifically testing foods and recipes for various packing manufacturers, as well as the same staff that helps |

| | | |
|---|---|---|
| Age 60-85 | 1948-1972 | her write her two books. Meta's books continue to be published and updated by her until they go out of publication in 1972. |
| Age 54-85 | 1942-1972 | Meta Given sells close to four million cookbooks with *The Modern Family Cook Book* being the most popular with two million plus copies in circulation and *The Encyclopedia of Modern Cooking* selling close to two million copies to the general public as well as universities picking it up as a text and reference book for home economic classes throughout the country. |
| 60-93 | 1948-81 | Meta Given leaves the Chicago area to semi-retire to Florida where she lives out her life in various towns. While there she enjoys the local fruits and vegetables incorporating them into new recipes for updates of her cookbooks. |
| Age 63-71 | 1951-59 | At retirement age for most of us, Meta Given's cookbook *The Modern Encyclopedia of Cooking* was published as one large volume for several years with over 1699 pages give or take an index |
| Age 87 | 1975 | Jane Nickerson retired Food Editor of the *New York Times* who is at that time the Food Editor for the *Ocala Star-Banner* and later at *Lakeland Ledger* interviews Meta Given. |
| Age 93 | 1981 | Meta Given dies at the age of 93 on November 17, 1981. |
| Age 93 | 1981 | Obituary listed in the *Lakeland Ledger* newspaper. Jane republishes the interview in 1981 after Meta Given dies. The tribute to Meta's life is prompted after Jane finds the obituary of Meta Given lacking in a proper tribute to this illustrious woman who brought modern-day cooking to the masses through her cookbooks and syndicated column about food on a budget. |
| Age 125 | 2013 | Danette Bishop Mondou starts researching Meta Given's story for a biography. |
| Age 130 | 2018 | *My Time with Meta Hortense Given: A Biography* written by Danette Bishop Mondou is published. |
| Age 130 | Future | Google Doodle for Meta Hortense Given (lol) predicted |

# Given Family Tree from 1693 – 1981

| | | | | |
|---|---|---|---|---|
| 1693-1740 | Samuel Given | Born Antrim Ulster County Ireland | Died Virginia Colony | 5th Great Grand father |
| 1719- | John Given | Born Antrim Ulster County Ireland | Died Virginia Colony | 4th Great Grand father |
| 1746-1792 | William Given | Born Virginia Colony | Died Virginia Colony | 3rd Great Grand father |
| 1773- | William Given II | Born Virginia Colony | Died Virginia Colony | 2nd Great Grand father |
| 1808-1887 | Henry Given | Born Virginia State | Died in Missouri State | Great Grand father |
| 1829- | John Given | Born in Virginia State | Died in Missouri State | Grand father |
| 1858-1920 | James Henry Given | Born Missouri State | Died in Missouri State | Father |
| 1888-1981 | Meta Hortense Given | Born in Missouri State | Died in Florida State | Self |

# Bibliography

*1888.* (1888, 12 23). Retrieved from wikipedia.

*1888.* (2017, 11 20). Retrieved from wikipedia: https://en.wikipedia.org/wiki/1888

2015 https://www.huffingtonpost.com/2015/03/27/ women-in-tech_n_6955940.html

*Abigail Adams.* (2017, 11 17). Retrieved from wikipedia: https://en.wikipedia.org/wiki/Abigail_Adams

Ad Fairbanks Morse Refrigerator. (1938, 01 20). *Cambridge City Tribune*, p. 4.

*Ada Lovelace.* (2017, 11 16). Retrieved from wikipedia: https://en.wikipedia.org/wiki/Ada_Lovelace

Alice Ross, L. C. (2017, 11 11). *Feeding America Project.* Retrieved from Cook Books: http://digital.lib.msu.edu/projects/cookbooks/html/museum.html

*Annie Jump Cannon.* (2017, 11 17). Retrieved from wikipedia: https://en.wikipedia.org/wiki/Annie_Jump_Cannon

*Apprenticeship in history.* (2017). Retrieved from ini.wa.gov: http://www.lni.wa.gov/TradesLicensing/Apprenticeship/About/History/

*Bella Abzug.* (2017, 11 17). Retrieved from wikipedia: https://en.wikipedia.org/wiki/Bella_Abzug

*Benjamin Franklin.* (2017, 12 20). Retrieved from americanlibrary.gov: http://www.americaslibrary.gov/aa/franklinb/aa_franklinb_printer_4.html

*Biographies Benjamin Frankin How I became a Printer in Philadelphia.* (2017, 12 22). Retrieved from let.rug.nl/usa/biographies: http://www.let.rug.nl/usa/biographies/benjamin-franklin/how-i-became-a-printer-in-philadelphia.php

Bishop, L. G. (2013, 07 05). Common Knowledge. Hodgdon, Maine, USA: Leola Gerow Bishop.

*Brighton Beach.* (2017, 11 25). Retrieved from wikipedia: https://en.wikipedia.org/wiki/Brighton_Beach and 1888 wikipedia

Brown, C. (1949, 05 12). Cook Goes into the Library. *The News*, p. 18.

by Gail Donaldson, U. C. (2017, 11 15). *Melanie Klein (1882-1960),* 2002 The Feminist Psychologist, Newsletter of the Society for the Psychology of Women. Retrieved 11 15, 2017, from apadivisions: http://www.apadivisions.org/division-35/about/heritage/melanie-klein-biography.aspx

Career of an Expert Cook. (1941, January 2). *St. Louis Post-Dispatch*, p. 24. Retrieved April 11, 2017, from file:///C:/Users/dennylou56/Documents/acer/MHG/meta%20givens/NewspapersArticles/STLouisDispatch/1941_01__Jan__02_St__Louis_Post_Dispatch_MO_Meta_Given_Bio_with_picturefullpage.pdf

*Casey at the Bat*. (2017, 11 25). Retrieved from wikipedia: https://en.wikipedia.org/wiki/Casey_at_the_Bat

Chakrabarti, M. (2017, 11 11). *Old Cookbooks Find A Home At Harvard*. Retrieved from Radcliff Harvard EDU: https://www.radcliffe.harvard.edu/news/in-news/old-cookbooks-find-home-harvard

Chakrabarti, M. (2017, 12 15). *Old cookbooks find home at harvard*. Retrieved from radcliff.harvard.edu: https://www.radcliffe.harvard.edu/news/in-news/old-cookbooks-find-home-harvard

*Chocolate*. (2017, 11 11). Retrieved from Wikipedia: https://en.wikipedia.org/wiki/Chocolate

*Depression 1929*. (2017, 12 13). Retrieved from SJSU.edu: http://www.sjsu.edu/faculty/watkins/dep1929.htm

Distinguished Food Authority to Write. (1943, 02 05). *Wisconsin State Journal*, p. 12.

Eddy, K. (1997, July 16). Serving Food News For 150 Years. *Chicago Tribune*. Chicago, Illinois, USA: Chicago Tribune. Retrieved January 10, 2016, from http://articles.chicagotribune.com/1997-07-16/entertainment/9707170320_1_food-page-pen-cake-mixes

*Ellen Swallow Richards*. (2017, 12 06). Retrieved from wikipedia: https://en.wikipedia.org/wiki/Ellen_Swallow_Richards

*Evelyn Beatrice Longman*. (2013, 07 05). Retrieved from wikipedia: https://en.wikipedia.org/wiki/Evelyn_Beatrice_Longman

*Evelyn Beatrice Longman*. (2017, 11 17). Retrieved from wikipedia: https://en.wikipedia.org/wiki/Evelyn_Beatrice_Longman

*Everyday Magazine: Career of an Expert Cook*. (1941, 01 02). Retrieved from newspapers.com: https://www.newspapers.com/image/137659046/?terms=%22Meta%2BGiven%22

Fane, V. (2017, 11 11). *Good Things come to those who wait*. Retrieved from wikipedia: https://en.wikipedia.org/wiki/Good_things_come_to_those_who_wait

*Feed America*. (2013, 11 25). Retrieved from digital.lib.msu.edu: http://digital.lib.msu.edu/projects/cookbooks/index.cfm

find source. (2017).

*Florene Ellinwood Allen.* (2017, 12 22). Retrieved from wikipedia: https://en.wikipedia.org/wiki/Florence_Ellinwood_Allen

Ford, H. (1924). *My life and Work.*

*Frank Julian Sprague.* (2017, 11 23). Retrieved from wikipedia: https://en.wikipedia.org/wiki/Frank_J._Sprague

*Frederick Douglass.* (2017, 11 25). Retrieved from wikipedia: https://en.wikipedia.org/wiki/Frederick_Douglass

Fugate, D. E. (1933, 09 04). 1933_09(Sep) 04 Married Women and Job in Lincoln Star, Lincoln, Nebraska page 6. *Lincoln Star*, p. 6.

*George Eastman Patents.* (2017, 11 25). Retrieved from wikipedia: https://en.wikipedia.org/wiki/George_Eastman#Patents

Gimbels Cooking School Directed by Meta Given. (1942, 04 12). *The Pittsburgh Press*, p. 3.

Given, M. (1930 - 1931). Food Talk. *Chicago Tribune.* Chicago, Illinois, USA: Chicago Tribune.

Given, M. (1930, 11 30). *Chicago Sunday Tribune Doughnuts, If rightly made, fluffy as cake.* Retrieved from Newspapers.com: https://www.newspapers.com/image/194971005/

Given, M. (1930, 06 10). *Food Talk.* Retrieved from newspapers.com: June 10, 1930, Chicago Tribune Food Talk by Meta Given page 33 (fix this)

Given, M. (1932, 08). *Botulinus KPoisoning in Home Canning Brochure Bulletin No. 5.* Retrieved 12 20, 2017, from ttu-ir.tdl.org: https://ttu-ir.tdl.org/ttu-ir/bitstream/handle/2346/45526/ttu_hcc001_000078.pdfoning%20in%20Home%20Canning%20Brochure%20MHG%20Bulletin%20no%205.pdf

Given, M. (1942). *Modern Family Cook book.* Chicago: J. G. Ferguson and Associates.

Given, M. (1943, 03 18). Ration Points Must Have Careful Study If Family Budget Is To Be Maintained. *Harrisburg Telegraph*, p. 12.

Given, M. (1947). *Meta Given's Encyclopedia of Cooking Cookbook* . Chicago: J. G. Ferguson and Associates.

Given, M. (1953). *Meta Given's Encyclopedia of Cooking* (1953 ed.). Chicago, IL: Ferguson. Retrieved 2016

Given, M. (2013, 10 31). *Milwaukee Sentinel.* Retrieved from Google Newspaper Archives: nolongerexists - taken down

*Great Blizzard of 1888.* (2017, 11 23). Retrieved from wikipedia: https://en.wikipedia.org/wiki/Great_Blizzard_of_1888

*Her Hat was in the Ring Biography*. (2017, 11 16). Retrieved from Her Hat was in the Ring: http://www.herhatwasinthering.org/biography.php?id=6283

Hickox, G. A. (1871). *Legal Disabilities of Married Women*. Retrieved from archive.org: https://archive.org/stream/legaldisabilitie00hick#page/n1/mode/2up

*History Joy Cooking*. (2017, 11 25). Retrieved from The Joy Kitchen: http://www.thejoykitchen.com/all-about-joy/history-joy-cooking

*https://en.wikipedia.org/wiki/Dorothy_Dix*. (2017, 12 20). Retrieved from wikipedia: https://en.wikipedia.org/wiki/Dorothy_Dix

Hughes, J. (Writer), & Dragoti, S. (Director). (1983). *Mr. Mom* [Motion Picture]. Retrieved from https://en.wikipedia.org/wiki/Mr._Mom

Introducing New Members. (1925, 02). *Chemical Bulletin*.

Introducing New Members. (1925). *The Chemical bulletin February, 1925 page 49*, 49.

*James Lick Telescope*. (2017, 11 20). Retrieved from wikipedia: https://en.wikipedia.org/wiki/James_Lick_telescope

Kroeger, B. (2013). *Nellie Bly: Daredevil. Reporter. Feminist.* Amazon.

*Leroy Buffington*. (2017, 11 23). Retrieved from on this day: https://www.onthisday.com/events/may/22

*Lillian Valborg Mariea Helander*. (2017, 11 16). Retrieved from askart: http://www.askart.com/artist/Lillian_Valborg_Mariea_Helander/10024239/Lillian_Valborg_Mariea_Helander.aspx

*Lily Haxworth Wallace*. (n.d.). Retrieved from biblio: https://www.biblio.com/lily-haxworth-wallace/author/1086

*Louisa May Alcott*. (2017, 11 23). Retrieved from wikipedia: https://en.wikipedia.org/wiki/Louisa_May_Alcott

LUTES, J. M. (2007). *FRONT-PAGE GIRLS: WOMEN JOURNALISTS IN AMERICAN CULTURE AND FICTION*. Ithaca: Cornell University Press.

*Marie Currie*. (2017, 11 16). Retrieved from wikipedia: https://en.wikipedia.org/wiki/Marie_Curie#Nobel_Prizes

*May Aufderheide*. (2017, 11 25). Retrieved from wikipedia: https://en.wikipedia.org/wiki/May_Aufderheide

Meta Given Has A New Kind of Cooking School. (1937, 11 25). *Oak Park Leaves*.

*Nellie Bly*. (2017, 11 16). Retrieved from wikipedia: HTTPS://EN.WIKIPEDIA.ORG/WIKI/NELLIE_BLY

News From A Field. (1917). *Journal of Home Economics*, 488. Retrieved from https://books.google.com/books?id=VmAVAAAAIAAJ&pg=PA488&lpg=PA488&dq=dr.+evelyn+g.halliday+home+economics&source=bl&ots=IbQMSUdAwq&sig=5A9vuEOhIx_HHcadtYwQmss5Ncg&hl=en&sa=X&ved=0ahUKEwjZ-OHf4p7XAhUTzGMKHbE9DgEQ6AEIKDAA#v=onepage&q=dr.%20evelyn%20g.hallid

Nickerson, J. (1975, 02 26). Cooking Encyclopedia Author Full of Information. *Ocala Star-Banner*. Ocala, Florida, USA: Ocala.

Nickerson, J. (2017, 12 18). *Ocala Star-Banner*. Retrieved from news google archives: https://news.google.com/newspapers?nid=hXZnTIgIr50C&dat=19750226&printsec=frontpage&hl=en

*Nicolas Appert*. (2017, 12 18). Retrieved from wikipedia: https://en.wikipedia.org/wiki/Nicolas_Appert

Numerous Articles. (1933-1949). *Various Newspapers*.

Patricia "Eddie" Edwards, P. P. (2008). *Antique Trader Collectible Cookbooks Price Guide*. Wisconsin: Krause Publication. Retrieved 2014, from https://books.google.com/books?id=FHVwD4-ONoUC&pg=PA94&lpg=PA94&dq=%22Meta+Given%22+%22Go-to-girl%22&source=bl&ots=4i7q8vkiD-&sig=QBob3m4fkszDdvHNpVUctbK5Kdc&hl=en&sa=X&ved=0ahUKEwiC9pyrz87XAhUJjFQKHeEoBqwQ6AEIKDAA#v=onepage&q=%22Meta%20Given%22%20%22Go-t

Patterson, H. L. (1922). *Patterson'sAmerican Educational Directory 19-24*. Retrieved from books.google.com: https://books.google.com/books?id=LgIVIf8S6qEC&pg=PA266&lpg=PA266&dq=Patterson's+School+Meta+Given&source=bl&ots=DGdfRQMvUQ&sig=9QuKAerp2Q9MQceZakn5a9Kuzc8&hl=en&sa=X&ved=0ahUKEwiBl9rcyZfYAhVDy2MKHRLEA9MQ6AEIQDAH#v=onepage&q=Patterson's%20School%20Meta%20

Phi U Apron Sale, Special. (1947, 11 07). *The Spectrum State College Station*, p. 1.

Reiter, J. S. (1978). *The Old West: The Women*. Time-Life Books.

Reiter, J. S. (1978). *THE OLD WEST: THE WOMEN*. TIME-LIFE BOOKS.

Sara Stage, V. B. (1997). *Rethinking Home Economics: Women and the History of a Profession*. Cornell: Cornell University Press.

*Schoolhouse Blizzard 1888*. (2017, 11 23). Retrieved from wikipedia: https://en.wikipedia.org/wiki/Schoolhouse_Blizzard

*Secret Ballot*. (2017, 11 23). Retrieved from wikipedia: https://en.wikipedia.org/wiki/Secret_ballot#United_States

*Seismometer*. (2017, 11 25). Retrieved from wikipedia:
https://en.wikipedia.org/wiki/Seismometer

Snyder, Thomas D. Editor, 120 years of American Education: A statistical Portrait.
(2018  https://www.statista.com/statistics/194675/us-book-production-by-subject-since-2002-cookery/

*Steve Jobs*. (2017, 11 15). Retrieved from Wikipedia:
https://en.wikipedia.org/wiki/Steve_Jobs

Sudermann, H. (2017, 12 09). *Washington State Magazine*. Retrieved from wsm.wsu.edu:
http://wsm.wsu.edu/s/index.php?id=265

*Susan B. Anthony*. (2017, 11 26). Retrieved from wnd.infobaselearning.com:
http://wnd.infobaselearning.com/wnd-encyclopedia.aspx?id=1018&rturl=Search+Results&search=Susan+B.+anthony+World+Women&option=1&oper=1&umbtype=2

Swaby, R. (2015). *HEADSTRONG: 52 WOMEN WHO CHANGED SCIENCE-AND THE WORLD*. New York, New York: Broadway Books Crown Publishing.

Swaby, R. (2015, 04 07). *Rachel Swaby*. Retrieved from amazon.com:
https://www.amazon.com/Rachel-Swaby/e/B00NVQ5EUQ/ref=dp_byline_cont_book_1

*The Joy of Cooking*. (2017, 11 16). Retrieved from wikipedia:
https://en.wikipedia.org/wiki/The_Joy_of_Cooking

*Thomas Edison*. (2017, 11 23). Retrieved from wikipedia:
https://en.wikipedia.org/wiki/Thomas_Edison

Thompson, D. (2011, 11 22). *The Amazing History and the Strange Invention of the Bendy Straw*. Retrieved from The Atlantic:
https://www.theatlantic.com/business/archive/2011/11/the-amazing-history-and-the-strange-invention-of-the-bendy-straw/248923/

*Tim Roaix*. (2017).

Tucker, A. (2017, 12 18). *Succotash Recipe with a History*. Retrieved from New England.com:
https://newengland.com/yankee-magazine/food/succotash-recipe-with-a-history/

Twain, M. (2017, 11 25). *The Gilded Age: A Tale of Today*. Retrieved from wikipedia:
https://en.wikipedia.org/wiki/The_Gilded_Age:_A_Tale_of_Today

Virginia Springs. (1856). *newspapers.com*,
https://www.newspapers.com/image/79772920/?terms=railway%2Band%2Bstages.

Walker, F. C. (1942, 04 14). *Pittsburgh Post-Gazette*. Retrieved 05 28, 2015, from newspapers.com: https://www.newspapers.com/image/90542949/?terms=%22Meta%2BGiven%22

West Virginians. (1856). *Richmond Dispatch*, page 2.

# Index

## A

Aufder Heide 19, 41, 42, 44, 45, 48, 49, 52, 53, 55, 56, 57, 58, 63, 64, 170

## B

Beecher ........ 68, 95, 96, 178, 186
Blacksmith .............................. 27
Bland, Missouri ...... 42, 44, 47, 55

## C

Chicago Tribune 50, 74, 182, 183, 203, 204, 205, 209, 210, 212, 213, 214, 215, 216, 217, 218, 242, 251, 252, 253, 259, 267, 270, 276, 277

## E

Enterprise School .................... 51
Evaporated Milk 34, 35, 38, 49, 138, 181, 194, 196, 201, 205, 249, 251, 253, 269, 270

## F

Feeding America .... 68, 87, 96, 99
Food Talk 50, 74, 182, 183, 204, 210, 211, 214, 270, 277

## G

Gasconade County 19, 40, 42, 48, 49, 50, 54, 56, 64, 269
Gasconade County Republican 48, 49, 50, 54, 56
Given, Ann ............................... 62
Given, Carrie .......................... 62
Given, James .................... 62, 269
Given, Meta ....................... 14, 49

## H

Hortense 19, 23, 33, 39, 77, 78, 79, 99, 162, 173, 191, 257, 259, 265, 268, 272, 273

## J

Joy of Cooking 72, 73, 80, 81, 94, 147, 152, 175, 248, 257, 281
Julie & Julia .................................. v

## K

Kindergarten ......................... 145

## L

Lakeland, Florida ..................... 65

## M

Meta Given's Encyclopedia of Cooking v, 54, 62, 98, 101, 149, 221, 238, 260, 261, 271
Michigan State University . 68, 87
Modern Family Cook Book 148, 221, 238, 245, 246, 248, 257, 258, 271

## O

Owensville 20, 34, 35, 41, 42, 43, 44, 45, 47, 48, 50, 51, 52, 55, 56, 57, 58
Owensville High School 42, 48, 52

## P

Principal ................... 8, 43, 48, 52

## R

Radcliffe College ...................... 72
Rethinking Home Economics 74, 280
Rumford Cookbook ................. 93

## S

Scientific Kitchen 47, 53, 69, 116, 157, 158, 219, 224, 247, 250, 271
Servant .................................. 88
St. Louis Dispatch ............ 78, 107
Stoves ...................................... 69

## T

Timeline .......................... vii, 269

Tribune Cook Book .. 74, 204, 210

## U

University of Chicago vii, 7, 29, 31, 32, 33, 35, 36, 37, 41, 93, 147, 174, 176, 194, 196, 197, 198, 201, 240, 241, 244, 249, 251, 255, 257, 258, 269, 270, 271
University of Missouri ........ 32, 40

Made in the USA
Lexington, KY
27 November 2018